The Green Tree Library

The Plays of Maurice Maeterlinck

SECOND SERIES

THE PLAYS

OF

Maurice Maeterlinck

SECOND SERIES

ALLADINE AND PALOMIDES · PÉL-
LÉAS AND MÉLISANDE · HOME ·
THE DEATH OF TINTAGILES

TRANSLATED BY

RICHARD HOVEY

HERBERT S. STONE & COMPANY
CHICAGO AND NEW YORK
MDCCCCII

COPYRIGHT, 1896, BY
STONE AND KIMBALL

Contents

Préface.

ON m'a demandé plus d'une fois si mes
drames, de *La Princesse Maleine* à *La
Mort de Tintagiles*, avaient été réellement écrits
pour un théâtre de marionettes, ainsi que je
l'avais affirmé dans l'édition originale de cette
sauvage petite légende des malheurs de Maleine.
En vérité, ils ne furent pas écrits pour des
acteurs ordinaires. Il n'y avait là nul désir
ironique et pas la moindre humilité non plus.
Je croyais sincèrement et je crois encore au-
jourd'hui, que les poèmes meurent lorsque des
êtres vivants s'y introduisent. Un jour, dans
un écrit dont je ne retrouve plus que quelques
fragments mutilés, j'ai essayé d'expliquer ces
choses qui dorment, sans doute, au fond de
notre instinct et qu'il est bien difficile de ré-
veiller complètement. J'y constatais d'abord,
qu'une inquiètude nous attendait à tout spectacle auquel nous assistions et qu'une déception
à peu près ineffable accompagnait toujours la
chute du rideau. N'est-il pas évident que le
Macbeth ou l'Hamlet que nous voyons sur
la scène ne ressemble pas au Macbeth ou à

l'Hamlet du livre? Qu'il a visiblement retro-
gradé dans le sublime? Qu'une grande partie
des efforts du poète qui voulait créer avant tout
une vie supérieure, une vie plus proche de
notre âme, a été annulée par une force ennemie
qui ne peut se manifester qu'en ramenant cette
vie supérieure au niveau de la vie ordinaire?
Il y a peut-être, me disais-je, aux sources de
ce malaise, un très ancien malentendu, à la
suite duquel le théâtre ne fut jamais exactement
ce qu'il est dans l'instinct de la foule, à savoir:
le temple du Rêve. Il faut admettre, ajoutai-je,
que le théâtre, du moins en ses tendances, est
un art. Mais je n'y trouve pas la marque des
autres arts. L'art use toujours d'un détour
et n'agit pas directement. Il a pour mission
suprême la révélation de l'infini et de la grandeur ainsi que la beauté secrète, de l'homme.
Mais montrer au doigt à l'enfant qui nous ac-
compagne, les étoiles d'une nuit de Juillet, ce
n'est pas faire une œuvre d'art. Il faut que
l'art agisse comme les abeilles. Elles n'apportent pas aux larves de la ruche les fleurs
des champs qui renferment leur avenir et leur
vie. Les larves mourraient sous ces fleurs sans
se douter de rien. Il faut que les abeilles nour-
ricières apportent à ces nymphes aveugles l'âme
même de ces fleurs, et c'est alors seulement
qu'elles trouveront sans le savoir en ce miel mys-

térieux la substance des ailes qui un jour les
emporteront à leur tour dans l'espace. Or, le
poème était une œuvre d'art et portait ces
obliques et admirables marques. Mais la repré-
sentation vient le contredire. Elle chasse vrai-
ment les cygnes du grand lac, et elle rejette les
perles dans l'abîme. Elle remet les choses
exactement au point où elles étaient avant
la venue du poète. La densité mystique de
l'œuvre d'art a disparue. Elle verse dans la
même erreur que celui qui après avoir vanté
à ses auditeurs l'admirable *Annonciation* de
Vinci, par exemple, s'imaginerait qu'il a fait
pénétrer dans leurs âmes la beauté surnaturelle
de cette peinture en reproduisant, en un tableau
vivant, tous les détails du grand chef-d'œuvre
florentin.

Qui sait si ce n'est pas pour ces raisons
cachées que l'on est obligé de s'avouer que
la plupart des grands poèmes de l'humanité ne
sont pas scéniques ? *Lear, Hamlet, Othello,
Macbeth, Antoine et Cléopâtre,* ne peuvent être
représentés, et il est dangereux de les voir sur
la scène. Quelque chose d'Hamlet est mort
pour nous du jour où nous l'avons vu mourir
sous nos yeux. Le spectre d'un acteur l'a
détrôné, et nous ne pouvons plus écarter l'usur-
pateur de nos rêves. Ouvrez les portes, ouvrez
le livre, le prince antérieur ne revient plus. Il

a perdu la faculté de vivre selon la beauté la plus
secrète de notre âme. Parfois son ombre passe
encore en tremblant sur le seuil, mais désormais
il n'ose plus, il ne peut plus entrer ; et bien des
voix sont mortes qui l'acclamaient en nous.

Je me souviens de cette mort de l'Hamlet de
mes rêves. Un soir j'ouvris la porte à l'usur-
pateur du poème. L'acteur était illustre. Il
entra. Un seul de ses regards me montra qu'il
n'était pas Hamlet. Il ne le fut pas un seul
instant pour moi. Je le vis s'agiter durant trois
heures dans le mensonge. Je voyais claire-
ment qu'il avait ses propres destinées ; et
celles qu'il voulait représenter m'étaient indi-
ciblement indifférentes à côté des siennes. Je
voyais sa santé et ses habitudes, ses passions et
ses tristesses, ses pensées et ses œuvres, et il
essayait vainement de m'intéresser à une vie
qui n'était pas la sienne et que sa seule présence avait rendue factice. Depuis je le revois
lorsque j'ouvre le livre et Elsinore n'est plus
le palais d'autrefois. . . .

"La vérité," dit quelque part Charles Lamb,
"la vérité est que les caractères de Shakespeare
sont tellement des objets de méditation plutôt
que d'intérêt ou de curiosité relativement à
leurs actes, que, tandis que nous lisons l'un
de ses grands caractères criminels, — Macbeth, Richard, Iago même, — nous ne songeons

pas tant aux crimes qu'ils commettent, qu'à
l'ambition, à l'esprit d'aspiration, à l'activité
intellectuelle qui les poussent à franchir ces
barrières morales. Les actions nous affectent
si peu, que, tandis que les impulsions, l'esprit
intérieur en toute sa perverse grandeur, pa-
raissent seuls réels et appellent seuls l'attention,
le crime n'est comparativement rien. Mais
lorsque nous voyons représenter ces choses, les
actes sont comparativement tout, et les mobiles
ne sont plus rien. L'émotion sublime où nous
sommes entraînés par ces images de nuit et
d'horreur qu'exprime Macbeth; ce solennel
prélude où il s'oublie jusqu'à ce que l'horloge
sonne l'heure qui doit l'appeler au meurtre de
Duncan; lorsque nous ne lisons plus cela dans
un livre, lorsque nous avons abandonné ce poste
avantageux de l'abstraction d'où la lecture
domine la vision, et lorsque nous voyons sous
nos yeux, un homme en sa forme corporelle se
préparer actuellement au meurtre; si le jeu de
l'acteur est vrai et puissant, la pénible anxiété
au sujet de l'acte, le naturel désir de le prévenir
tout qu'il ne semble pas accompli, la trop puis-
sante apparence de réalité, provoquent un malaise et une inquiétude qui détruisent totalement
le plaisir que les mots apportent dans le livre,
où l'acte ne nous oppresse jamais de la pénible
sensation de sa présence, et semble plutôt appar-

tenir à l'histoire ; à quelque chose de passé et
d'inévitable.''

Charles Lamb a raison, et pour mille raisons
bien plus profondes encore que celles qu'il nous
donne. Le théâtre est le lieu où meurent la plupart des chefs-d'œuvre, parce que la représen-
tation d'un chef-d'œuvre à l'aide d'éléments
accidentels et humains est antinomique. Tout
chef-d'œuvre est un symbole, et le symbole ne
supporte pas la présence active de l'homme. Il
suffit que le coq chante, dit Hamlet, pour que
les spectres de la nuit s'évanouissent. Et de
même, le poème perd sa vie "de la seconde
sphère" lorsqu'un être de la sphère inférieure
s'y introduit. L'accident ramène le symbole à
l'accident ; et le chef-d'œuvre, en son essence,
est mort durant le temps de cette présence et
de ses traces.

Les Grecs n'ignorèrent pas cette antinomie, et
leurs masques que nous ne comprenons plus,
ne servaient probablement qu'à atténuer la
présence de l'homme et à soulager le symbole.
Aux époques où le théâtre eut une vie véritable,
il la dût peut-être uniquement à quelque cir-
constance ou à quelque artifice qui venait en
aide du poème dans sa lutte contre l'homme.
Ainsi, sous Elisabeth, par exemple, la déclama-
tion était une sorte de mélopée, le jeu était
conventionnel, et la scène aussi. Il en était à

peu près de même sous Louis XIV. Le poème
se retire à mesure que l'homme s'avance. Le
poème veut nous arracher du pouvoir de nos
sens et faire prédominer le passé et l'avenir ;
l'homme, au contraire, n'agit que sur nos sens et
n'existe que pour autant qu'il puisse effacer cette
prédomination. S'il entre en scène avec toutes
ses puissances, et libre comme s'il entrait dans
une forêt ; si sa voix, ses gestes, et son attitude
ne sont pas voilées par un grand nombre de con-
ventions synthétiques ; si l'on aperçoit un seul
instant l'être vivant qu'il est et l'âme qu'il
possède, — il n'y a pas de poème au monde qui
ne recule devant lui. A ce moment précis, le
spectacle du poème s'interrompt et nous assis-
tons à une scène de la vie extérieure, qui, de
même qu'une scène de la rue, de la rivière, ou
du champ de bataille, a ses beautés éternelles
et secrètes, mais qui est néanmoins impuissante
à nous arracher du présent, parce qu'en cet
instant nous n'avons pas la qualité pour aperce-
voir ces beautés invisibles, qui ne sont que "des
fleurs offertes aux vers aveugles."

Et c'est pour ces raisons, et pour d'autres
encore qu'on pourrait rechercher dans les
mêmes parages, que j'avais destiné mes petits
drames à des êtres indulgents aux poèmes, et
que, faute de mieux, j'appelle "Marionettes."

Maurice Maeterlinck.

Alladine and Palomides.

To Camille Mauclair.

Persons.

ABLAMORE.

ASTOLAINE, *daughter of Ablamore.*

ALLADINE.

PALOMIDES.

THE SISTERS OF PALOMIDES.

A PHYSICIAN.

[NOTE: The translation of Ablamore's song is taken from the version of this play made by the editors of "Poet-lore."   R. H.]

Alladine and Palomides.

———◆———

ACT FIRST.

A wild part of the gardens. ABLAMORE *discovered leaning over* ALLADINE, *who is asleep.*

ABLAMORE.

Methinks sleep reigns day and night beneath these trees. Each time she comes here with me toward nightfall, she is hardly seated when she falls asleep. Alas! I must be glad even of that. . . . During the day, whene'er I speak to her and her look happens to encounter mine, it is hard as a slave's to whom a thing impossible has just been bidden. . . . Yet that is not her customary look. . . . I have seen her many times resting her beautiful eyes on children, on the forest, the sea, or her surroundings. She smiles at me as one smiles on a foe; and I dare not bend over her save at times when her eyes can no longer see me. . . . I have a few moments every evening; and all the rest of the day I live beside her with my eyes cast down. . . . It is sad to love too late. . . . Maids

cannot understand that years do not separate
hearts. . . . They have called me "The wise
King." . . . I was wise because till now nothing
had happened to me. . . . There are men who
seem to turn events aside. It was enough that
I should be about for nothing to be able to
have birth. . . . I had suspected it of old. . . .
In the time of my youth, I had many friends
whose presence seemed to attract every adven-
ture; but the days when I went forth with
them, for the encounter of joys or sorrows, they
came back again with empty hands. . . . I
think I palsied fate; and I long took pride in
this gift. One lived under cover in my reign.
. . . But now I have recognized that misfortune
itself is better worth than sleep, and that there
must be a life more active and higher than
waiting. . . . They shall see that I too have
strength to trouble, when I will, the water that
seems dead at the bottom of the great caldrons
of the future. . . . Alladine, Alladine! . . .
Oh! she is lovely so, her hair over the flowers
and over her pet lamb, her lips apart and
fresher than the morn. . . . I will kiss her
without her knowing, holding back my poor
white beard. . . . [*He kisses her.*] — She
smiled. . . . Should I pity her? For the few
years she gives me, she will some day be queen;
and I shall have done a little good before I go
away. . . . They will be astonished. . . . She
herself does not know. . . . Ah! here she
wakes with a start. . . . Where are you coming
from, Alladine?

ALLADINE.

I have had a bad dream. . . .

ABLAMORE.

What is the matter? Why do you look yonder?

ALLADINE.

Some one went by upon the road.

ABLAMORE.

I heard nothing.

ALLADINE.

I tell you some one is coming. . . . There he is! [*She points out a young knight coming forward through the trees and holding his horse by the bridle.*] Do not take me by the hand; I am not afraid. . . . He has not seen us. . . .

ABLAMORE.

Who dares come here? . . . If I did not know . . . I believe it is Palomides. . . . It is Astolaine's betrothed. . . . He has raised his head. . . . Is it you, Palomides?

Enter PALOMIDES.

PALOMIDES.

Yes, my father . . . If I am suffered yet to call you by that name . . . I come hither before the day and the hour. . . .

ABLAMORE.

You are a welcome guest, whatever hour it be.
. . . But what has happened? We did not
expect you for two days yet. . . . Is Astolaine
here, too? . . .

PALOMIDES.

No; she will come to-morrow. We have
journeyed day and night. She was tired and
begged me to come on before. . . . Are my
sisters come?

ABLAMORE.

They have been here three days waiting
for your wedding. — You look very happy,
Palomides. . . .

PALOMIDES.

Who would not be happy, to have found
what he sought? I was sad of old. But now
the days seem lighter and more sweet than
harmless birds in the hand. . . . And if old
moments come again by chance, I draw near
Astolaine, and you would think I threw a
window open on the dawn. . . . She has a soul
that can be seen around her, — that takes you
in its arms like an ailing child and without saying anything to you consoles you for everything.
. . . I shall never understand it at all. — I do
not know how it can all be; but my knees bend
in spite of me when I speak of it. . . .

ALLADINE.

I want to go in again.

ABLAMORE.

[*Seeing that* ALLADINE *and* PALOMIDES *look at each other stealthily.*] This is little Alladine who has come hither from the heart of Arcady. . . . Take hands. . . Does that astonish you, Palomides? . . .

PALOMIDES.

My father . . .
    [PALOMIDES' *horse starts aside, frightening*
      ALLADINE'S *lamb.*]

ABLAMORE.

Take care. . . . Your horse has frightened Alladine's lamb. . . . He will run away. . . .

ALLADINE.

No; he never runs away. . . . He has been startled, but he will not run away. . . . It is a lamb my godmother gave me. . . . He is not like others. . . . He stays beside me night and day.   [*Caressing it.*

PALOMIDES (*also caressing it*).

He looks at me with the eyes of a child. . . .

ALLADINE.

He understands everything that happens. . . .

ABLAMORE.

It is time to go find your sisters, Palomides.
. . . They will be astonished to see you. . . .

ALLADINE.

They have gone every day to the turning of
the road. . . . I have gone with them; but
they did not hope yet. . . .

ABLAMORE.

Come; Palomides is covered with dust, and
he must be weary. . . . We have too many
things to say to each other to talk here. . . . We
will say them to-morrow. . . . They claim the
morn is wiser than the evening. . . . I see the
palace gates are open and seem to wait for
us. . . .

ALLADINE.

I cannot help being uneasy when I go back
into the palace. . . . It is so big, and I am so
little, and I get lost there still. . . . And then all
those windows on the sea. . . . You cannot
count them. . . . And the corridors that turn
without reason, and others that never turn, but
lose themselves between the walls. . . . And
the halls I dare not go into. . . .

PALOMIDES.

We will go in everywhere. . . .

ALLADINE.

You would think I was not made to dwell
there, — that it was not built for me. . . .

Once I lost my way there. . . . I pushed open thirty doors, before I found the light of day again. . . . And I could not go out; the last door opened on a pool. . . . And the vaults that are cold all summer; and the galleries that bend back on themselves endlessly. . . . There are stairways that lead nowhere and terraces from which nothing can be seen. . . .

ABLAMORE.

You who were not wont to talk, how you talk to-night ! . . .

[*Exeunt.*

ACT SECOND.

SCENE **I.** — ALLADINE *discovered, her forehead against one of the windows that open on the park. Enter* ABLAMORE.

ABLAMORE.

Alladine. . . .

ALLADINE (turning abruptly).

What is it?

ABLAMORE.

Oh, how pale you are ! . . . Are you ill?

ALLADINE.

No.

ABLAMORE.

What is it in the park? — Were you looking at the avenue of fountains that unfolds before your windows? — They are wonderful and weariless. They were raised there one by one, at the death of each of my daughters. . . . At night I hear them singing in the garden. . . . They bring to mind the lives they represent, and I can tell their voices apart. . . .

ALLADINE.

I know.

ABLAMORE.

You must pardon me; I sometimes repeat the same things and my memory is less trustworthy. . . . It is not age; I am not an old man yet, thank God! but kings have a thousand cares. Palomides has been telling me his adventures. . . .

ALLADINE.

Ah!

ABLAMORE.

He has not done what he would; young people have no will any more. — He astonishes me. I had chosen him among a thousand for my daughter. He should have had a soul as deep as hers. — He has done nothing which may not be excusable, but I had hoped more. . . . What do you say of him?

ALLADINE.

Who?

ABLAMORE.

Palomides?

ALLADINE.

I have only seen him one evening. . . .

ABLAMORE.

He astonishes me. — Everything has succeeded with him till now. He would undertake a thing and accomplish it without a word. — He would get out of danger without an effort, while others could not open a door without finding death behind it. — He was of those whom events seem to await on their knees. But a little while ago something snapped. You would say he has no longer the same star, and every step he takes carries him further from himself. — I don't know what it is. — He does not seem to be at all aware, but others can remark it. . . . Let us speak of something else: look! the night comes; I see it rise along the walls. Would you like to go together to the wood of Astolat, as we do other evenings?

ALLADINE.

I am not going out to-night.

ABLAMORE.

We will stay here, since you prefer it so. Yet the air is sweet and the evening very fair. [ALLADINE *starts without his noticing it.*] I have had flowers set along the hedges, and I should like to show them to you. . . .

ALLADINE.

No, not to-night. . . . If you wish me to . . . I like to go there with you . . . the air is pure and the trees . . . but not to-night. . . . [*Cowers, weeping, against the old man's breast.*] I do not feel quite well. . . .

ABLAMORE.

What is the matter? You are going to fall. . . . I will call. . . .

ALLADINE.

No, no. . . . It is nothing. . . . It is over. . . .

ABLAMORE.

Sit down. Wait. . . .

> [He runs to the folding-doors at the back and opens both. Palomides is seen, seated on a bench. He has not had time to turn away his eyes. Ablamore looks fixedly at him, without a word, then re-enters the room. Palomides rises and retreats in the corridor, stifling the sound of his footsteps. The pet lamb leaves the room, unperceived.]

SCENE II. — *A drawbridge over the moats of the palace.* PALOMIDES *and* ALLADINE, *with her pet lamb, appear at the two ends of the bridge.* KING ABLAMORE *leans out from a window of the tower.*

PALOMIDES.

Were you going out, Alladine? — I was coming in.   I am coming back from the chase. — It rained.

ALLADINE.

I have never passed this bridge.

PALOMIDES.

It leads to the forest. It is seldom passed. People had rather go a long way around. I think they are afraid because the moats are deeper at this place than elsewhere, and the black water that comes down from the moun-

tains boils horribly between the walls before it
goes hurling itself into the sea. It roars there
always ; but the quays are so high you hardly
notice it. It is the most deserted wing of the
palace. But on this side the forest is more
beautiful, more ancient, and greater than any
you have seen. It is full of unusual trees and
flowers that have sprung up of themselves. —
Will you come?

ALLADINE.

I do not know. . . . I am afraid of the
roaring water.

PALOMIDES.

Come, come ; it roars without reason. Look
at your lamb ; he looks at me as if he wished
to come. . . . Come, come. . . .

ALLADINE.

Don't call him. . . . He will get away.

PALOMIDES.

Come, come.
[The lamb escapes from Alladine's hands, and
comes leaping toward Palomides, but slips
on the inclined plane of the drawbridge and
goes rolling into the moat.]

ALLADINE.

What has he done? —Where is he?

PALOMIDES.

He slipped. He is struggling in the heart of
the eddy. Do not look at him ; there is nothing to be done. . . ,

ALLADINE.

You are going to save him?

PALOMIDES.

Save him? But look! he is already in the tunnel. One moment more, and he will be under the vaults; and God himself will never see him more. . . .

ALLADINE.

Go away!   Go away!

PALOMIDES.

What is the matter?

ALLADINE.

Go away! — I do not want to see you any more! . . .

> [Ablamore enters precipitately, seizes Alladine, and draws her away brusquely without speaking.]

SCENE III. — *A room in the palace.* ABLA-
MORE *and* ALLADINE *discovered*.

ABLAMORE.

You see, Alladine, my hands do not tremble, my heart beats like a sleeping child's, and my voice has not once been stirred with wrath. I bear no ill-will to Palomides, although what he has done might seem unpardonable. And as for thee, who could bear thee ill-will? You obey laws you do not know, and you could not

2

act otherwise.   I will not speak to you of what took place the other day along the palace moats, nor of all the unforeseen death of the lamb might have revealed to me, had I believed in omens for an instant.   But last night I surprised the kiss you gave each other under the windows of Astolaine.   At that moment I was with her in her room.   She has a soul that fears so much to trouble, with a tear or with a simple movement of her eyelids, the happiness of those about her, that I shall never know if she, as I, surprised that wretched kiss.   But I know what she has the power to suffer.   I shall not ask you anything you cannot avow to me, but I would know if you had any secret design in following Palomides under the window where you must have seen us.   Answer me without fear;   you know beforehand I will pardon everything.

ALLADINE.

I did not kiss him.

ABLAMORE.

What?   You did not kiss Palomides, and Palomides did not kiss you?

ALLADINE.

No.

ABLAMORE.

Ah! . . . Listen : I came here to forgive you everything. . . . I thought you had acted as we almost all act, without aught of our soul in-

tervening. . . . But now I will know all that
passed. . . . You love Palomides, and you have
kissed him under my eyes. . . .

ALLADINE.

No.

ABLAMORE.

Don't go away. I am only an old man. Do
not flee. . . .

ALLADINE.

I am not fleeing.

ABLAMORE.

Ah! ah! You do not flee, because you
think my old hands harmless! They have yet
the strength to tear a secret out in spite of all.
[*He seizes her arms.*] And they could wrestle
with all those you prefer. . . . [*He twists her
arms behind her head.*] Ah! you will not
speak! . . . There will yet come a time when
all your soul shall spirt out like a clear spring,
for woe. . . .

ALLADINE.

No, no!

ABLAMORE.

Again, . . . we are not at the end, the journey
is very long — and naked truth is hid among
the rocks. . . . Will she come forth? . . . I
see her gestures in your eyes already, and her
cool breath will lave my visage soon. . . . Ah!
. . . Alladine! Alladine! . . . [*He releases her
suddenly.*] I heard your bones cry out like

little children. . . . I have not hurt you? . . .
Do not stay thus, upon your knees before me.
. . . It is I who go down on my knees. [*He
does as he says.*] I am a wretch. . . . You
must have pity. . . . It is not for myself alone
I pray. . . . I have only one poor daughter.
. . . All the rest are dead. . . . I had seven
of them about me. . . . They were fair and full
of happiness ; and I saw them no more. . . .
The only one left to me is going to die, too.
. . . She did not love life. . . . But one day
she encountered something she no longer looked
for, and I saw she had lost the desire to die.
. . . I do not ask a thing impossible. . . .

[ALLADINE *weeps and makes no answer.*

SCENE IV. — *The apartment of* ASTOLAINE.
ASTOLAINE *and* PALOMIDES *discovered.*

PALOMIDES.

Astolaine, when I met you several months
ago by chance, it seemed to me that I had
found at last what I had sought for during many
years. . . . Till you, I did not know all that
the ever tenderer goodness and complete sim-
plicity of a high soul might be. I was so deeply
stirred by it that it seemed to me the first time
I had met a human being. You would have
said that I had lived till then in a closed chamber which you opened for me ; and all at once
I knew what must be the soul of other men and

what mine might become. . . . Since then,
I have known you further. I have seen you
act, and others too have taught me all that you
have been.

There have been evenings when I quitted
you without a word, and went to weep for won-
der in a corner of the palace, because you had
simply raised your eyes, made a little uncon-
scious gesture, or smiled for no apparent cause,
yet at the moment when all the souls about you
asked it and would be satisfied. There is but
you who know these moments, because you are,
it seems, the soul of all, and I do not believe
those who have not drawn near you can know
what true life is. To-day I come to say all this
to you, because I feel that I shall never be
he whom I hoped once to become. . . . A
chance has come — or haply I myself have
come ; for you can never tell if you have made
a movement of yourself, or if it be chance that
has met with you. — a chance has come, which
has opened my eyes, just as we were about to
make each other unhappy ; and I have recognized there must be something more incompre-
hensible than the beauty of the most beautiful
soul or the most beautiful face ; and mightier,
too, since I must needs obey it. . . . I do not
know if you have understood me. If you
understand, have pity on me. . . . I have said
to myself all that could be said. . . . I know
what I shall lose, for I know her soul is a child's
soul, a poor strengthless child's, beside yours,
and yet I cannot resist it. . . .

ASTOLAINE.

Do not weep. . . . I know too that one does
not do what one would do . . . nor was I igno-
rant that you would come. . . . There must
indeed be laws mightier than those of our souls,
of which we always speak. . . . [*Kissing him
abruptly*]. — But I love thee the more, my poor
Palomides.

PALOMIDES.

I love thee, too . . . more than her I love.
. . . Thou weepest, as I do?

ASTOLAINE.

They are little tears. . . . Do not be sad for
them. . . . I weep so, because I am woman,
but they say our tears are not painful. . . .
You see I can dry them already. . . . I knew
well what it was. . . . I waited for the waken-
ing. . . . It has come; and I can breathe with
less disquietude, being no longer happy. . . .
There ! . . . We must see clearly now for you
and her. For I believe my father already has
suspicions.   [*Exeunt*.

ACT THIRD.

SCENE I. — *A room in the palace.* ABLAMORE
discovered. ASTOLAINE *stands on the step of
a half-open door at the back of the hall.*

ASTOLAINE.

Father, I have come because a voice that I
no longer can resist, commands me to. I told
you all that happened in my soul when I met
Palomides. He was not like other men. . . .
To-day I come to ask your help . . . for I do
not know what should be said to him. . . .
I have become aware I cannot love him. . . .
He has remained the same, and I alone have
changed, or have not understood. . . . And
since it is impossible for me to love, as I have
dreamed of love, him I had chosen among
all, it must be that my heart is shut to these
things. . . . I know it to-day. . . . I shall look
no more toward love; and you will see me
living on about you without sadness and without unrest. . . . I feel that I am going to be
happy. . . .

ABLAMORE.

Come hither, Astolaine. It is not so that
you were wont to speak in the old days to
your father. You wait there, on the threshold
of a door hardly ajar, as if you were ready to

flee ; and with your hand upon the key, as if you would close from me forever the secret of your heart. You know quite well I have not understood what you have just said, and that words have no sense when souls are not within reach of each other. Draw nearer still, and speak no more to me. [ASTOLAINE *approaches slowly.*] There is a moment when souls touch each other, and know all without need that one should move the lips. Draw nearer. . . . They do not reach each other yet, and their radiance is so slight about us ! . . . [ASTOLAINE *stops.*] Thou darest not? — Thou knowest too how far one can go? — It is I who must. . . . [*He approaches Astolaine with slow steps, then stops and looks long at her.*] I see thee, Astolaine. . . .

ASTOLAINE.

Father ! . . . [*She sobs as she kisses the old man.*]

ABLAMORE.

You see well it was useless. . . .

SCENE II. — *A chamber in the palace.*

Enter ALLADINE *and* PALOMIDES.

PALOMIDES.

All will be ready to-morrow. We cannot wait longer. He prowls like a madman through the corridors of the palace ; I met him even

now. He looked at me without a word. I
passed; and as I turned, I saw him slyly laugh,
shaking his keys. When he perceived that I
was looking at him, he smiled at me, making
signs of friendship. He must have some secret
project, and we are in the hands of a master
whose reason begins to totter. . . . To-morrow
we shall be far away. . . . Yonder there are
wonderful countries that resemble thine. . . .
Astolaine has already provided for our flight
and for my sisters'. . . .

ALLADINE.

What has she said?

PALOMIDES.

Nothing, nothing. . . . You will see everything about my father's castle, — after days of
sea and days of forests — you will see lakes and
mountains . . . not like these, under a sky that
looks like the vault of a cave, with black trees
that the storms destroy . . . but a sky beneath
which there is nothing more to fear, — forests that
are always awake, flowers that do not close. . . .

ALLADINE.

She wept?

PALOMIDES.

What are you asking? . . . There is something
there of which we have no right to speak, do you
understand? . . . There is a life there that does
not belong to our poor life, and which love has
no right to approach except in silence. . . . We

are here, like two beggars in rags, when I
think of it. . . Go! go! . . . I could tell you
things. . . .

ALLADINE.

Palomides! . . . What is the matter?

PALOMIDES.

Go! go! . . . I have seen tears that came
from further than the eyes. . . . There is something else. . . . It may be, nevertheless, that
we are right . . . but how I regret being right
so, my God! . . . Go! . . . I will tell you to-
morrow . . . to-morrow . . . to-morrow. . . .
[*Exeunt severally.*

SCENE III. — *A corridor before the apartment
of* ALLADINE. *Enter* ASTOLAINE *and the* SIS-
TERS OF PALOMIDES.

ASTOLAINE.

The horses wait in the forest, but Palomides
will not flee; and yet your lives and his are
in danger. I do not know my poor father
any longer. He has a fixed idea that troubles
his reason. This is the third day I have followed him step by step, hiding myself behind
the pillars and the walls, for he suffers no one
to companion him. To-day, as the other days,
and from the first gleams of the morning he
has gone wandering through the corridors and
halls of the palace, and along the moats and

ramparts, shaking the great golden keys he has had made and singing at the top of his voice the strange song whose refrain, *Go follow what your eyes have seen*, has perhaps pierced even to the depths of your chambers. I have concealed from you till now all that has come to pass, because such things must not be spoken of without reason. He must have shut up Alladine in this apartment, but no one knows what he has done with her. I have listened at the doors every night and whenever he has been away a moment, but I have never heard any noise in the room. . . . Do you hear anything?

ONE OF THE SISTERS OF PALOMIDES.

No; I hear only the murmur of the air passing through the little chinks of the wood. . . .

ANOTHER SISTER.

It seems to me, when I listen hard, that I hear the great pendulum of the clock.

A THIRD SISTER.

But what is this little Alladine, then, and why does he bear such ill-will to her?

ASTOLAINE.

It is a little Greek slave that came from the heart of Arcady. . . . He bears her no ill-will, but . . . Do you hear? — It is my father. . . . [*Singing heard in the distance.*] Hide yourselves behind the pillars. . . He will have no one pass by this corridor. — [*They hide.*]

Enter ABLAMORE, *singing and shaking a bunch of great keys.*

ABLAMORE (*sings*).

Misfortune had three golden keys.
— He has no rescue for the Queen! —
Misfortune had three golden keys.
Go follow what your eyes have seen.

[Sits dejected on a bench, beside the door of
Alladine's apartment, hums a little while
longer, and soon goes to sleep, his arms
hanging down and his head fallen.]

ASTOLAINE.

Come, come! make no noise. He has fallen asleep on the bench. — Oh, my poor old
father! How white his hair has grown during
these days! He is so weak, he is so unhappy,
that sleep itself no longer brings him peace.
It is three whole days now since I have dared to
look upon his face. . . .

ONE OF THE SISTERS OF PALOMIDES.

He sleeps profoundly. . . .

ASTOLAINE.

He sleeps profoundly, but you can see his
soul has no rest. . . . The sunlight here will vex
his eyelids. . . . I am going to draw his cloak
over his face. . . .

ANOTHER SISTER.

No, no; do not touch it. . . . He might wake with a start. . . .

ASTOLAINE.

Some one is coming in the corridor. Come, come! put yourselves before him. . . . Hide him. . . . A stranger must not see him in this state. . . .

A SISTER OF PALOMIDES.

It is Palomides. . . .

ASTOLAINE.

I am going to cover his poor eyes. . . . [*She covers* ABLAMORE'S *face.*] — I would not have Palomides see him thus. . . . He is too miserable.

Enter PALOMIDES.

PALOMIDES.

What is the matter?

ONE OF THE SISTERS.

He has fallen asleep on the bench.

PALOMIDES.

I have followed him without his seeing me. . . . He said nothing? . . .

ASTOLAINE.

No; but see all he has suffered. . . .

PALOMIDES.

Has he the keys?

ANOTHER SISTER.

He holds them in his hand. . . .

PALOMIDES.

I am going to take them.

ASTOLAINE.

What are you going to do? Oh, do not
wake him! . . . For three nights now he has
wandered through the palace. . . .

PALOMIDES.

I will open his hand a little without his noticing it. . . . We have no right to wait any
longer. . . . God knows what he has done.
. . . He will forgive us when he has his reason
back. . . . Oh! oh! his hand has no strength
any more. . . .

ASTOLAINE.

Take care! Take care!

PALOMIDES.

I have the keys.—Which is it? I am going
to open the room.

ONE OF THE SISTERS.

Oh, I am afraid! . . . Do not open it at
once. . . . Palomides! . . .

PALOMIDES.

Stay here. . . . I do not know what I shall
find. . . .
 [*He goes to the door, opens it, and enters the
 apartment.*

ASTOLAINE.

Is she there?

PALOMIDES (*in the apartment*).

I cannot see. . . . The shutters are closed. . . .

ASTOLAINE.

Have a care, Palomides. . . . Wilt thou that
I go first? . . . Thy voice is trembling. . . .

PALOMIDES (*in the apartment*).

No, no. . . . I see a ray of sunlight falling
through the chinks of the shutters.

ONE OF THE SISTERS.

Yes; it is broad day out of doors.

PALOMIDES.

[*Rushing headlong from the room.*] Come!
Come! . . . I think she . . .

ASTOLAINE.

Thou hast seen her? . . .

PALOMIDES.

She is stretched out on the bed! . . . She
does not stir! . . . I do not think she . . .
Come! Come! [*They all go into the room.*

ASTOLAINE AND THE SISTERS OF PALOMIDES.

[*In the room.*]   She is here. . . . No, no,
she is not dead. . . . Alladine ! Alladine ! . . .
Oh ! oh !   The poor child ! . . . Do not cry
out so. . . . She has fainted. . . . Her hair is
tied across her mouth. . . . And her hands are
bound behind her back. . . . They are bound
with the help of her hair. . . . Alladine ! Alladine ! . . . Fetch some water. . . .

> [ABLAMORE, *who has waked, appears on the
> step of the door.*

ASTOLAINE.

There is my father ! . . .

ABLAMORE (*going to* PALOMIDES).

Was it you who opened the door of the room ?

PALOMIDES.

Yes, it was I. . . . I did it — well, then ?
— well, then ? . . . I could not let her die
under my eyes. . . . See what you have done.
Alladine ! . . . Fear nothing. . . . She opens
her eyes a little. . . . I will not . . .

ABLAMORE.

Do not cry out. . . . Do not cry out so. . . .
Come, we will open the shutters. . . . You cannot see here.   Alladine ! . . . She is already
sitting up.   Alladine, come too. . . . Do you
see, my children, it is dark in the room.   It is
as dark here as if we were a thousand feet under
the ground.   But I open one of the shutters,

and behold ! All the light of the sky and the
sun ! . . . It does not need much effort; the
light is full of good-will. . . . It suffices that
one call it; it always obeys. . . . Have you
seen the river with its little islands between the
meadows in flower? . . . The sky is a crystal
ring to-day. . . . Alladine ! Palomides, come
see. . . . Draw both of you near Paradise. . . .
You must kiss each other in the new light. . . .
I bear you no ill-will. You did what was
ordained; and so did I. . . . Lean out a moment from the open window, and look once
more at the sweet green things. . . .

    [*A silence. He closes the shutter without
      a word.*

ACT FOURTH.

Vast subterranean crypts.   ALLADINE *and*
PALOMIDES.

PALOMIDES.

They have bound my eyes with bands; they
have tied my hands with cords.

ALLADINE.

They have tied my hands with cords; they
have bound my eyes with bands. . . . I think
my hands are bleeding. . . .

PALOMIDES.

Wait.   To-day I bless my strength. . . . I
feel the knots beginning to give way. . . . One
struggle more, and let my fists burst!   One
struggle more!   I have my hands!   [*Tearing
away the bandage.*]   And my eyes! . . .

ALLADINE.

You see now?

PALOMIDES.

Yes.

ALLADINE.

Where are we?

PALOMIDES.

Where are you?

ALLADINE.

Here; can you not see me?

PALOMIDES.

My eyes weep still where the band has left
its trace. . . . We are not in darkness. . . .
Is it you I hear toward where I can just see?

ALLADINE.

I am here; come.

PALOMIDES.

You are at the edge of that which gives us light.
Do not stir; I cannot see all that there is about
you. My eyes have not forgot the bandage yet.
They bound it tight enough to burst my eyelids.

ALLADINE.

Come; the knots stifle me. I can wait no
longer. . . .

PALOMIDES.

I hear only a voice coming out of the
light. . . .

ALLADINE.

Where are you?

PALOMIDES.

I have no idea myself. I walk still in darkness. . . . Speak again, that I may find you.

You seem to be on the edge of an unbounded light. . . .

ALLADINE.

Come ! come ! I have borne without a word, but I can bear no more. . . .

PALOMIDES (*groping forward*).

You are there? I thought you so far away ! . . . My tears deceived me. I am here, and I see you. Oh, your hands are wounded ! They have bled upon your gown, and the knots have entered into the flesh. I have no longer any weapons. They have taken away my poniard. I will tear them off. Wait ! wait ! I have the knots.

ALLADINE.

Take off the bandage first that makes me blind. . . .

PALOMIDES.

I cannot. . . . I do not see. . . . It seems to be surrounded by a net of golden threads.   . .

ALLADINE.

My hands, then, my hands !

PALOMIDES.

They have taken silken cords. . . . Wait, the knots come undone. The cord has thirty turns. . . . There, there ! — Oh, your hands are all blood ! . . . You would say they were dead. . . .

ALLADINE.

No, no ! . . . They are alive ! they are alive !
See ! . . .

> [With her hands hardly yet unbound, she clasps
> Palomides about the neck and kisses him
> passionately.]

PALOMIDES.

Alladine !

ALLADINE.

Palomides !

PALOMIDES.

Alladine, Alladine ! . . .

ALLADINE.

I am happy ! . . . I have waited a long
while ! . . .

PALOMIDES.

I was afraid to come. . . .

ALLADINE.

I am happy . . . and I would that I could
see thee. . . .

PALOMIDES.

They have tied down the bandage like a
casque. . . .— Do not turn round; I have
found the golden threads. . . .

ALLADINE.

Yes, yes, I will turn round. . . .

> [*She turns about, to kiss him again.*

PALOMIDES.

Have a care. Do not stir. I am afraid of wounding thee. . . .

ALLADINE.

Tear it away! Fear nothing. I can bear no more! . . .

PALOMIDES.

I would see thee too. . . .

ALLADINE.

Tear it away! Tear it away! I am no longer within reach of woe! . . . Tear it away! . . . Thou dost not know that one could wish to die. . . . Where are we?

PALOMIDES.

Thou 'lt see, thou 'lt see. . . . It is innumerable crypts . . . great blue halls, gleaming pillars, and deep vaults. . . .

ALLADINE.

Why dost thou answer when I question thee?

PALOMIDES.

What matter where we be, if we be but together? . . .

ALLADINE.

Thou lovest me less already?

PALOMIDES.

Why, what ails thee?

ALLADINE.

I know well where I am when I am on thy heart. . . . Oh, tear the bandage off! . . . I would not enter blind into thy soul. . . . What doest thou, Palomides? Thou dost not laugh when I laugh. Thou dost not weep when I weep. Thou dost not clap thy hands when I clap mine ; and thou tremblest not when I speak trembling to the bottom of my soul. . . . The band! The band! . . . I will see! . . . There, there, above my hair! . . . [*She tears away the bandage.*] Oh! . . .

PALOMIDES.

Seest thou?

ALLADINE.

Yes. . . . I see thee only. . . .

PALOMIDES.

What is it, Alladine? Thou kissest me as if thou wert already sad. . . .

ALLADINE.

Where are we?

PALOMIDES.

Why dost thou ask so sadly?

ALLADINE.

No, I am not sad ; but my eyes will hardly open. . . .

PALOMIDES.

One would say your joy had fallen on my
lips like a child at the threshold of the house.
. . . Do not turn away. . . . I fear lest you
should flee, and I fear lest I dream. . . .

ALLADINE.

Where are we?

PALOMIDES.

We are in crypts that I have never seen. . . .
Doth it not seem to thee the light increases?
When I unclosed my eyes, I could distinguish
nothing; now little by little it is all revealed.
I have been often told of wondrous caverns
whereon the halls of Ablamore were built. It
must be these. No one descends here ever;
and the king only has the keys. I knew the
sea flooded the lowest vaults; and it is probably the reflex of the sea which thus illumines
us. . . . They thought to bury us in night.
They came down here with torches and flam-
beaus and saw the darkness only, while the
light came out to meet us, seeing we had none.
. . . It brightens without ceasing. . . . I am
sure the dawn pierces the ocean and sends
down to us through all its greening waves the
purest of its child-soul. . . .

ALLADINE.

How long have we been here?

PALOMIDES.

I have no idea. . . . I made no effort till I heard thee speak. . . .

ALLADINE.

I do not know how this took place. I was asleep in the room where thou didst find me; and when I waked, my eyes were bound across, and both my hands were pinioned in my girdle. . . .

PALOMIDES.

I too was sleeping. I heard nothing, and I had a band across my eyes ere I could open them. I struggled in the darkness; but they were stronger than I. . . . I must have passed under deep vaults, for I felt the cold fall on my shoulders; and I went down so far I could not count the steps. . . . Did no one speak to thee?

ALLADINE.

No; no one spoke. I heard some one weeping as he walked; and then I fainted. . . .

PALOMIDES (*kissing her*).

Alladine!

ALLADINE.

How gravely thou dost kiss me! . . .

PALOMIDES.

Close not thine eyes when I do kiss thee so. . . . I would see the kisses trembling in

thy heart, and all the dew that rises in thy
soul. . . . We shall not find such kisses any
more. . . .

ALLADINE.

Always, always !

PALOMIDES.

No, no ; there is no kissing twice upon the
heart of death. . . . How fair thou art so ! . . .
It is the first time I have seen thee near. . . .
It is strange, we think that we have seen each
other because we have gone by two steps apart ;
but everything changes the moment the lips
touch. . . . There, thou must be let to have thy
will. . . . I stretch my arms wide to admire thee,
as if thou wert no longer mine ; and then I
draw them nearer till I touch thy kisses and
perceive only eternal bliss. . . . There needed
us this supernatural light ! . . . [*He kisses her
again.*] Ah ! What hast thou done? Take
care ! we are upon a crest of rock that overhangs the water that gives us light. Do not
step back. It was time. . . . Do not turn too
abruptly. I was dazzled. . . .

ALLADINE.

[*Turning and looking at the blue water that
illuminates them.*] Oh ! . . .

PALOMIDES.

It is as if the sky had flowed hither. . . .

ALLADINE.

It is full of moveless flowers. . . .

PALOMIDES.

It is full of moveless flowers and strange. . . .
Hast thou seen the largest there that blooms
beneath the others?   It seems to live a
cadenced life. . . . And the water . . . Is it
water? . . . It seems more beautiful, more
pure, more blue than all the water in the
world. . . .

ALLADINE.

I dare not look upon it longer. . . .

PALOMIDES.

See how about us all is luminous. . . . The
light dares hesitate no longer, and we kiss each
other in the vestibules of heaven. . . . Seest
thou the precious stones that gem the vaults,
drunken with life, that seem to smile on us;
and the thousands and thousands of glowing
blue roses that climb along the pillars? . . .

ALLADINE.

Oh ! . . . I heard ! . . .

PALOMIDES.

What?

ALLADINE.

Some one striking the rocks. . . .

PALOMIDES.

No, no; it is the golden gates of a new Paradise, that open in our souls and sing upon their hinges! . . .

ALLADINE.

Listen . . . again, again! . . .

PALOMIDES (*with voice suddenly changed*).

Yes; it is there. . . . It is at the bottom of the bluest vaults. . . .

ALLADINE.

They are coming to. . . .

PALOMIDES.

I hear the sound of iron on the rock. . . . They have walled up the door or cannot open it. . . . It is the picks grating against the stone. . . . His soul has told him we were happy. . . .

> [A silence; then a stone is detached at the very end of the vault, and a ray of daylight breaks into the cavern.]

ALLADINE.

Oh! . . .

PALOMIDES.

It is another light. . . .

> [Motionless and anxious, they watch other stones detach themselves slowly in an insufferable light, and fall one by one; while the light, entering in more and more resistless floods, reveals to them little by little the gloom of the cavern they had thought mar-

vellous. The miraculous lake becomes wan
and sinister; the precious stones about them
are extinguished, and the glowing roses appear as the stains and rotten rubbish that they
are. At last, the whole side of rock falls
abruptly into the crypt. The sunlight enters,
dazzling. Calls and songs are heard without. Alladine and Palomides recoil.]

PALOMIDES.

Where are we?

ALLADINE (*embracing him*).

I love thee still, Palomides. . . .

PALOMIDES.

I love thee too, my Alladine. . . .

ALLADINE.

They come. . . .

PALOMIDES.

[*Looking behind him as they still recoil.*]
Have a care. . . .

ALLADINE.

No, no; have no more care. . . .

PALOMIDES (*looking at her*).

Alladine?

ALLADINE.

Yes. . .
[They still recoil before the invasion of light or
peril, until they lose their footing; and they
fall and disappear behind the rock that overhangs the underground and now gloomy
water. — A silence. Astolaine and the sisters
of Palomides enter the crypt.]

ASTOLAINE.

Where are they?

ONE OF THE SISTERS OF PALOMIDES.

Palomides ! . . .

ASTOLAINE.

Alladine ! Alladine ! . . .

ANOTHER SISTER.

Palomides ! . . . It is we ! . . .

THIRD SISTER.

Fear nothing ; we are alone ! . . .

ASTOLAINE.

Come ! come ! we have come to rescue you ! . . .

FOURTH SISTER.

Ablamore has fled. . . .

FIFTH SISTER.

He is no longer in the palace. . . .

SIXTH SISTER.

They do not answer. . . .

ASTOLAINE.

I heard the water stirred ! . . . This way, this way !

[*They run to the rock that overlooks the underground water.*]

ONE OF THE SISTERS.

They are there! . . .

ANOTHER SISTER.

Yes, yes; at the very bottom of the black
water. . . . They embrace.

THIRD SISTER.

They are dead.

FOURTH SISTER.

No, no; they are alive! they are alive! . . .
See. . . .

THE OTHER SISTERS.

Help! help! . . . Call! . . .

ASTOLAINE.

They make no effort to save themselves! . . .

ACT FIFTH.

[A corridor, so long that its furthest arches seem to lose themselves in a kind of indoor horizon. The sisters of Palomides wait before one of the innumerable closed doors that open into this corridor. They seem to be guarding it. A little further down, on the opposite side, Astolaine and the Physician converse before another door, also closed.]

ASTOLAINE.

[*To the Physician.*] Nothing has ever happened until now in this palace, where all things have seemed to be asleep since my sisters died; and my poor old father, pursued by a strange restlessness, has fretted without reason at this calm, which seems, for all that, the least dangerous form of happiness. Some time ago, — his reason beginning to totter even then, — he went up to the top of a high tower; and as he stretched his arms out timidly toward the forests and toward the sea, he said to me — smiling a little fearfully at his words, as if to disarm my incredulous smile — that he called about us events which had long been hidden beneath the horizon. They have come, alas! sooner and more in number than he expected, and a few days have sufficed for them to reign in his stead. He has been their first victim. He fled to the meadows, singing, all in tears, the evening when he had little Alladine and luckless Palomides taken down into the crypts. He has not since been seen. I have had search made everywhere throughout the country and even on the sea. He has not been found. At least, I had hoped to save those he made suffer unwittingly, for he has always been the tenderest of men and the best of fathers; but there, too, I think I came too late. I do not know what happened. They have not spoken yet. They doubtless must have thought, hearing the sound of the iron and seeing all at once the light again, that my father had regretted the kind of surcease he had granted them, and that some one came to bring them death. Or else they slipped as they drew back, upon the rock that overhangs the lake; and so must have fallen through heedlessness. But the water is not deep in that spot, and we succeeded in saving them without difficulty. To-day it is you alone who can do the rest.

[THE SISTERS OF PALOMIDES *have drawn nearer.*

THE PHYSICIAN.

They are both ailing with the same disease, and it is a disease I do not know. — But I have little hope left. They were seized perhaps with the cold of the underground waters; or else those waters may be poisonous. The decomposed body of Alladine's lamb was found there. — I will come back to-night. — Meanwhile they must have silence. . . . The level of life is very low in their hearts. . . . Do not go into their rooms and do not speak to them, for the least word, in the state they are in, might cause their death. . . . They must succeed in forgetting one another.   [*Exit.*

ONE OF THE SISTERS OF PALOMIDES.

I see that he will die.

ASTOLAINE.

No, no. . . . Do not weep; . . . one does not die so, at his age. . . .

ANOTHER SISTER.

But why is your father angry without reason at my poor brother?

THIRD SISTER.

I think your father loved Alladine.

ASTOLAINE.

Do not speak so of it. . . . He thought I suffered. He thought to have done good, and he did evil unwittingly. . . . That often happens to us. . . . It is my fault, perhaps. . . . I recall it to-day. . . . One night I was asleep. I was weeping in a dream. . . . We have little courage when we dream. I waked. . . . He was beside my bed, looking at me. . . . Perhaps he was deceived. . . .

FOURTH SISTER (*running*).

Alladine has stirred a little in her room. . . .

ASTOLAINE.

Go to the door . . . listen. . . . Perhaps it was the nurse rising. . . .

FIFTH SISTER (*listening at the door*).

No, no; I hear the nurse walking. . . . There is another noise.

SIXTH SISTER (*also running*).

I think Palomides has moved too ; I hear the murmur of a voice seeking. . . .

THE VOICE OF ALLADINE.

[*Very feebly, within the room.*] Palomides ! . . .

ONE OF THE SISTERS.

She is calling him ! . . .

ASTOLAINE.

Let us be careful ! . . . Go, go in front of the door, that Palomides may not hear. . . .

THE VOICE OF ALLADINE.

Palomides !

ASTOLAINE.

My God ! My God ! Silence that voice ! . . . Palomides will die of it if he hear it ! . . .

THE VOICE OF PALOMIDES.

[*Very feebly, within the other room.*]   Alladine ! . . .

ONE OF THE SISTERS.

He answers ! . . .

ASTOLAINE.

Three among you remain here . . . and we will go to the other door.   Come, come quickly. We will surround them.   We will try to defend them. . . . Lie back against the doors. . . . Perhaps they will hear no longer. . . .

ONE OF THE SISTERS.

I shall go into Alladine's room. . . .

SECOND SISTER.

Yes, yes ; prevent her from crying out again.

THIRD SISTER.

She is already cause of all this evil. . . .

ASTOLAINE.

Do not go in, or I go in to Palomides. . . . She also had a right to life ; and she has done nought but to live. . . . But that we cannot stifle in their passage their deadly words ! . . . We are without help, my poor sisters, my poor sisters, and hands cannot stop souls ! . . .

THE VOICE OF ALLADINE.

Palomides, is it thou?

THE VOICE OF PALOMIDES.

Where art thou, Alladine?

THE VOICE OF ALLADINE.

Is it thou whom I hear far from me making moan?

THE VOICE OF PALOMIDES.

Is it thou whom I hear calling, and see thee not?

THE VOICE OF ALLADINE.

One would believe thy voice had lost the last of hope. . . .

THE VOICE OF PALOMIDES.

One would believe that thine had crossed the winds of death. . . .

THE VOICE OF ALLADINE.

It goes hard with thy voice to pierce into my room. . . .

THE VOICE OF PALOMIDES.

And I no longer hear thy voice as of old time.

THE VOICE OF ALLADINE.

I have been woe for thee ! . . .

THE VOICE OF PALOMIDES.

They have divided us, but I do love thee ever. . . .

THE VOICE OF ALLADINE.

I have been woe for thee. . . . Art thou still suffering?

THE VOICE OF PALOMIDES.

No; I no longer suffer, but I fain would see thee. . . .

THE VOICE OF ALLADINE.

We shall not see each other more; the doors are shut. . . .

THE VOICE OF PALOMIDES.

Thy voice would make one say thou lovedst me no more. . . .

THE VOICE OF ALLADINE.

Yes, yes; I love thee still, but it is mournful now. . . .

THE VOICE OF PALOMIDES.

Whither is thy face turned? I hardly understand thee. . . .

THE VOICE OF ALLADINE.

We seem to be an hundred leagues from one another. . . .

THE VOICE OF PALOMIDES.

I try to rise in vain; my spirit is too heavy. . . .

THE VOICE OF ALLADINE.

I too would come, — I too, — but still my head falls back. . . .

THE VOICE OF PALOMIDES.

Thou seemest almost to speak in tears despite thyself. . . .

THE VOICE OF ALLADINE.

No; I wept long ago; it is no longer tears. . . .

THE VOICE OF PALOMIDES.

There's something in thy thoughts thou dost not tell me of. . . .

THE VOICE OF ALLADINE.

They were not precious stones. . . .

THE VOICE OF PALOMIDES.

And the flowers were not real. . . .

ONE OF THE SISTERS OF PALOMIDES.

They rave. . . .

ASTOLAINE.

No, no; they know what they are saying. . . .

THE VOICE OF ALLADINE.

It was the light that had no pity on us. . . .

THE VOICE OF PALOMIDES.

Where goest thou, Alladine? Thou 'rt being borne away. . . .

THE VOICE OF ALLADINE.

I have no more regret to lose the light o' the sun. . . .

THE VOICE OF PALOMIDES.

Yes, yes; we shall behold the sweet green things again! . . .

THE VOICE OF ALLADINE.

I have lost desire to live. . . .

[*A silence ; then more and more faintly :*]

THE VOICE OF PALOMIDES.

Alladine! . . .

THE VOICE OF ALLADINE.

Palomides! . . .

· THE VOICE OF PALOMIDES.

Alla . . . dine! . . .

[A silence. — Astolaine and the sisters of Palomides listen, in anguish. Then the nurse
opens, from the inside, the door of Palomides'
room, appears on the sill, makes a sign, and
all enter the room. The door closes behind
them. A new silence. A little afterwards,
the door of Alladine's room opens in its
turn; the other nurse comes out in like
manner, looks about in the corridor, and,
seeing no one, re-enters the room, leaving the
door wide open.]

[CURTAIN.]

Pélléas and Mélisande.

To Octave Mirbeau.
In witness of deep friendship,
admiration, and gratitude.

M. M.

Persons.

ARKËL, *King of Allemonde.*

GENEVIÈVE, *mother of Pélléas and Golaud.*

PÉLLÉAS,
GOLAUD, } *grandsons of Arkël.*

MÉLISANDE.

LITTLE YNIOLD, *son of Golaud (by a former marriage).*

A PHYSICIAN.

THE PORTER.

Servants, Beggars, etc.

Pélléas and Mélisande.

—◆—

ACT FIRST.

Scene I. — *The gate of the castle.*

Maidservants (*within*).

Open the gate ! Open the gate !

Porter (*within*).

Who is there? Why do you come and wake me up? Go out by the little gates; there are enough of them ! . . .

A Maidservant (*within*).

We have come to wash the threshold, the gate, and the steps; open, then ! open !

Another Maidservant (*within*).

There are going to be great happenings !

Third Maidservant (*within*).

There are going to be great fêtes ! Open quickly ! . . .

THE MAIDSERVANTS.

Open! open!

PORTER.

Wait! wait!   I do not know whether I shall be able to open it; . . . it is never opened. . . . Wait till it is light. . . .

FIRST MAIDSERVANT.

It is light enough without; I see the sunlight through the chinks. . . .

PORTER.

Here are the great keys. . . . Oh! oh! how the bolts and the locks grate! . . . Help me! help me! . . .

MAIDSERVANTS.

We are pulling; we are pulling. . . .

SECOND MAIDSERVANT.

It will not open. . . .

FIRST MAIDSERVANT.

Ah! ah! It is opening! it is opening slowly!

PORTER.

How it shrieks! how it shrieks! It will wake up everybody. . . .

SECOND MAIDSERVANT.

[*Appearing on the threshold.*]   Oh, how light it is already out-of-doors!

FIRST MAIDSERVANT.

The sun is rising on the sea !

PORTER.

It is open. . . . It is wide open ! . . .
[*All the maidservants appear on the threshold and pass over it.*]

FIRST MAIDSERVANT.

I am going to wash the sill first. . . .

SECOND MAIDSERVANT.

We shall never be able to clean all this.

OTHER MAIDSERVANTS.

Fetch the water ! fetch the water !

PORTER.

Yes, yes ; pour on water ; pour on water ; pour
on all the water of the Flood !   You will never
come to the end of it. . . .

SCENE II. — *A forest.* MÉLISANDE *discovered at
the brink of a spring.*

Enter GOLAUD.

GOLAUD.

I shall never be able to get out of this forest
again. — God knows where that beast has led
me.   And yet I thought I had wounded him to

death ; and here are traces of blood. But now I have lost sight of him ; I believe I am lost myself — my dogs can no longer find me — I shall retrace my steps. . . . — I hear weeping . . . Oh ! oh ! what is there yonder by the water's edge ? . . . A little girl weeping by the water's edge ? [*He coughs.*] — She does not hear me. I cannot see her face. [*He approaches and touches* MÉLISANDE *on the shoulder.*] Why weepest thou ? [MÉLISANDE *trembles, starts up, and would flee.*] — Do not be afraid. You have nothing to fear. Why are you weeping here all alone ?

MÉLISANDE.

Do not touch me ! do not touch me !

GOLAUD.

Do not be afraid. . . . I will not do you any. . . . Oh, you are beautiful !

MÉLISANDE.

Do not touch me ! do not touch me ! or I throw myself in the water ! . . .

GOLAUD.

I will not touch you. . . . See, I will stay here, against the tree. Do not be afraid. Has any one hurt you ?

MÉLISANDE.

Oh ! yes ! yes ! yes ! . . . [*She sobs profoundly.*]

GOLAUD.

Who has hurt you?

MÉLISANDE.

Every one! every one!

GOLAUD.

What hurt have they done you?

MÉLISANDE.

I will not tell!   I cannot tell! . . .

GOLAUD.

Come; do not weep so.   Whence come you?

MÉLISANDE.

I have fled! . . . fled . . . fled. . . .

GOLAUD.

Yes; but whence have you fled?

MÉLISANDE.

I am lost! . . . lost! . . . Oh! oh! lost here. . . . I am not of this place. . . . I was not born there. . . .

GOLAUD.

Whence are you?   Where were you born?

MÉLISANDE.

Oh! oh! far away from here! . . . far away . . . far away. . . .

5

GOLAUD.

What is it shining so at the bottom of the
water?

MÉLISANDE.

Where?— Ah! it is the crown he gave me.
It fell as I was weeping. . . .

GOLAUD.

A crown?— Who was it gave you a crown?
— I will try to get it. . . .

MÉLISANDE.

No, no; I will have no more of it! I will
have no more of it! . . . I had rather die . . .
die at once. . . .

GOLAUD.

I could easily pull it out. The water is not
very deep.

MÉLISANDE.

I will have no more of it! If you take it
out, I throw myself in its place! . . .

GOLAUD.

No, no; I will leave it there. It could be
reached without difficulty, nevertheless. It
seems very beautiful.— Is it long since you
fled?

MÉLISANDE.

Yes, yes! . . . Who are you?

GOLAUD.

I am Prince Golaud, — grandson of Arkël, the old King of Allemonde. . . .

MÉLISANDE.

Oh, you have gray hairs already. . . .

GOLAUD.

Yes ; some, here, by the temples . . .

MÉLISANDE.

And in your beard, too. . . . Why do you look at me so?

GOLAUD.

I am looking at your eyes. — Do you never shut your eyes?

MÉLISANDE.

Oh, yes ; I shut them at night. . . .

GOLAUD.

Why do you look so astonished?

MÉLISANDE.

You are a giant?

GOLAUD.

I am a man like the rest. . . .

MÉLISANDE.

Why have you come here?

GOLAUD.

I do not know, myself. I was hunting in the forest. I was chasing a wild boar. I mistook the road. — You look very young. How old are you?

MÉLISANDE.

I am beginning to be cold. . . .

GOLAUD.

Will you come with me !

MÉLISANDE.

No, no ; I will stay here. . . .

GOLAUD.

You cannot stay here all alone. You cannot stay here all night long. . . . What is your name?

MÉLISANDE.

Mélisande.

GOLAUD.

You cannot stay here, Mélisande. Come with me. . . .

MÉLISANDE.

I will stay here. . . .

GOLAUD.

You will be afraid, all alone. We do not know what there may be here . . . all night long . . . all alone . . . it is impossible. Mélisande, come, give me your hand. . . .

MÉLISANDE.

Oh, do not touch me ! . . .

GOLAUD.

Do not scream. . . . I will not touch you again. But come with me. The night will be very dark and very cold. Come with me. . . .

MÉLISANDE.

Where are you going? . . .

GOLAUD.

I do not know. . . . I am lost too. . . .

[*Exeunt.*

SCENE III. — *A hall in the castle.* ARKËL *and* GENEVIÈVE *discovered.*

GENEVIÈVE.

Here is what he writes to his brother Pélléas : " I found her all in tears one evening, beside a spring in the forest where I had lost myself. I do not know her age, nor who she is, nor whence she comes, and I dare not question her, for she must have had a sore fright ; and when you ask her what has happened to her, she falls at once a-weeping like a child, and sobs so heavily you are afraid. Just as I found her by the springs, a crown of gold had slipped from her hair and fallen to the bottom of the water. She was clad, besides, like a princess, though her garments had been torn by the briers. It is now six months since I married her and I know no more about it than on the day of our meeting. Meanwhile, dear Pélléas, thou whom I love more than a brother, although we were not born of the same father; meanwhile make ready for my return. . . . I know my mother will willingly forgive me. But I am afraid of the King, our venerable grandsire, I am afraid of Arkël, in spite of all his kindness, for I have undone by this strange marriage all his plans of state, and I fear the beauty of Mélisande will not excuse my folly to eyes so wise as his. If he consents nevertheless to receive her as he would receive his own daughter, the third night following this letter, light a lamp at the top of the tower that overlooks the sea. I shall perceive it from the bridge of our ship; otherwise I shall go far away again and come back no more. . . ." What say you of it?

ARKËL.

Nothing. He has done what he probably must have done. I am very old, and nevertheless I have not yet seen clearly for one moment into myself; how would you that I judge what others have done? I am not far from the tomb and do not succeed in judging myself. . . . One always mistakes when one does not close his eyes. That may seem strange to us; but that is all. He is past the age to marry and he weds, like a child, a little girl he finds by a spring. . . . That may seem strange to us,

because we never see but the reverse of destinies . . . the reverse even of our own. . . .
He has always followed my counsels hitherto;
I had thought to make him happy in sending him to ask the hand of Princess Ursula.
. . . He could not remain alone; since the death of his wife he has been sad to be alone;
and that marriage would have put an end to long wars and old hatreds. . . . He would not have it so. Let it be as he would have it; I have never put myself athwart a destiny; and he knows better than I his future. There happen perhaps no useless events. . . .

GENEVIÈVE.

He has always been so prudent, so grave and so firm. . . . If it were Pélléas, I should understand. . . . But he . . . at his age. . . . Who is it he is going to introduce here? — An unknown found along the roads. . . . Since his wife's death, he has no longer lived for aught but his son, the little Yniold, and if he were about to marry again, it was because you had wished it. . . . And now . . . a little girl in the forest. . . . He has forgotten everything. . . .
— What shall we do? . . .

Enter PÉLLÉAS.

ARKËL.

Who is coming in there?

GENEVIÈVE.

It is Pélléas. He has been weeping.

ARKËL.

Is it thou, Pélléas? — Come a little nearer,
that I may see thee in the light. . . .

PÉLLÉAS.

Grandfather, I received another letter at the
same time as my brother's; a letter from my
friend Marcellus. . . . He is about to die and
calls for me. He would see me before
dying. . . .

ARKËL.

Thou wouldst leave before thy brother's
return? — Perhaps thy friend is less ill than he
thinks. . . .

PÉLLÉAS.

His letter is so sad you can see death between
the lines. . . . He says he knows the very day
when death must come. . . . He tells me I can
arrive before it if I will, but that there is no
more time to lose. The journey is very long,
and if I await Golaud's return, it will be perhaps too late. . . .

ARKËL.

Thou must wait a little while, nevertheless.
. . . We do not know what this return has in
store for us. And besides, is not thy father
here, above us, more sick perhaps than thy
friend. . . . Couldst thou choose between the
father and the friend? . . .   [*Exit.*

·GENEVIÈVE.

Have a care to keep the lamp lit from this evening, Pélléas. . . .

[*Exeunt severally.*

SCENE IV. — *Before the castle.   Enter* GENE-
VIÈVE *and* MÉLISANDE.

MÉLISANDE.

It is gloomy in the gardens.   And what forests, what forests all about the palaces ! . . .

GENEVIÈVE.

Yes ; that astonished me too when I came hither ; it astonishes everybody.   There are places where you never see the sun.   But one gets used to it so quickly. . . . It is long ago, it is long ago. . . . It is nearly forty years that I have lived here. . . . Look toward the other side, you will have the light of the sea. . . .

MÉLISANDE.

I hear a noise below us. . . .

GENEVIÈVE.

Yes ; it is some one coming up toward us. . . . Ah ! it is Pélléas. . . . He seems still tired from having waited so long for you. . . .

MÉLISANDE.

He has not seen us.

GENEVIÈVE.

I think he has seen us but does not know what he should do. . . . Pélléas, Pélléas, is it thou? . . .

Enter PÉLLÉAS.

PÉLLÉAS.

Yes! . . . I was coming toward the sea. . . .

GENEVIÈVE.

So were we; we were seeking the light. It is a little lighter here than elsewhere; and yet the sea is gloomy.

PÉLLÉAS.

We shall have a storm to-night. There has been one every night for some time, and yet it is so calm now. . . . One might embark unwittingly and come back no more.

MÉLISANDE.

Something is leaving the port. . . .

PÉLLÉAS.

It must be a big ship. . . . The lights are very high, we shall see it in a moment, when it enters the band of light. . . .

GENEVIÈVE.

I do not know whether we shall be able to see it . . . there is still a fog on the sea. . . .

PÉLLÉAS.

The fog seems to be rising slowly. . . .

MÉLISANDE.

Yes; I see a little light down there, which I had not seen. . . .

PÉLLÉAS.

It is a lighthouse; there are others we cannot see yet.

MÉLISANDE.

The ship is in the light. . . . It is already very far away. . . .

PÉLLÉAS.

It is a foreign ship. It looks larger than ours. . . .

MÉLISANDE.

It is the ship that brought me here! . . .

PÉLLÉAS.

It flies away under full sail. . . .

MÉLISANDE.

It is the ship that brought me here. It has great sails. . . . I recognized it by its sails.

PÉLLÉAS.

There will be a rough sea to-night.

MÉLISANDE.

Why does it go away to-night? . . . You can hardly see it any longer. . . . Perhaps it will be wrecked. . . .

PÉLLÉAS.

The night falls very quickly. . . .

[A silence.

GENEVIÈVE.

No one speaks any more? . . . You have nothing more to say to each other? . . . It is time to go in. Pélléas, show Mélisande the way. I must go see little Yniold a moment.

[Exit.

PÉLLÉAS.

Nothing can be seen any longer on the sea. . . .

MÉLISANDE.

I see more lights.

PÉLLÉAS.

It is the other lighthouses. . . . Do you hear the sea? . . . It is the wind rising. . . . Let us go down this way. Will you give me your hand?

MÉLISANDE.

See, see, my hands are full. . . .

PÉLLÉAS.

I will hold you by the arm, the road is steep and it is very gloomy there. . . . I am going away perhaps to-morrow. . . .

MÉLISANDE.

Oh! . . . why do you go away?

[Exeunt.

ACT SECOND.

SCENE I. — *A fountain in the park.*

Enter PÉLLÉAS *and* MÉLISANDE.

PÉLLÉAS.

You do not know where I have brought you?
— I often come to sit here, toward noon, when
it is too hot in the gardens. It is stifling to-day,
even in the shade of the trees.

MÉLISANDE.

Oh, how clear the water is ! . . .

PÉLLÉAS.

It is as cool as winter. It is an old abandoned spring. It seems to have been a miraculous spring, — it opened the eyes of the blind,
— they still call it " Blind Man's Spring."

MÉLISANDE.

It no longer opens the eyes of the blind?

PÉLLÉAS.

Since the King has been nearly blind himself,
no one comes any more. . . .

MÉLISANDE.

How alone one is here! . . . There is no
sound.

PÉLLÉAS.

There is always a wonderful silence here. . . .
One could hear the water sleep. . . . Will you
sit down on the edge of the marble basin?
There is one linden where the sun never
comes. . . .

MÉLISANDE.

I am going to lie down on the marble. — I
should like to see the bottom of the water. . . .

PÉLLÉAS.

No one has ever seen it. — It is as deep,
perhaps, as the sea. — It is not known whence
it comes. — Perhaps it comes from the bottom
of the earth. . . .

MÉLISANDE.

If there were anything shining at the bottom,
perhaps one could see it. . . .

PÉLLÉAS.

Do not lean over so. . . .

MÉLISANDE.

I would like to touch the water. . . .

PÉLLÉAS.

Have a care of slipping. . . . I will hold
your hand. . . .

MÉLISANDE.

No, no, I would plunge both hands in it. . . .
You would say my hands were sick to-day. . . .

PÉLLÉAS.

Oh ! oh ! take care ! take care ! Mélisande !
. . . Mélisande ! . . . — Oh ! your hair ! . . .

MÉLISANDE (*starting upright*).

I cannot, . . . I cannot reach it. . . .

PÉLLÉAS.

Your hair dipped in the water. . . .

MÉLISANDE.

Yes, it is longer than my arms. . . . It is
longer than I. . . .   [*A silence.*

PÉLLÉAS.

It was at the brink of a spring, too, that he
found you?

MÉLISANDE.

Yes. . . .

PÉLLÉAS.

What did he say to you?

MÉLISANDE.

Nothing ; — I no longer remember. . . .

PÉLLÉAS.

Was he quite near you?

MÉLISANDE.

Yes; he would have kissed me.

PÉLLÉAS.

And you would not?

MÉLISANDE.

No.

PÉLLÉAS.

Why would you not?

MÉLISANDE.

Oh! oh! I saw something pass at the bottom of the water. . . .

PÉLLÉAS.

Take care! take care! — You will fall! What are you playing with?

MÉLISANDE.

With the ring he gave me. . . .

PÉLLÉAS.

Take care; you will lose it. . . .

MÉLISANDE.

No, no; I am sure of my hands. . . .

PÉLLÉAS.

Do not play so, over so deep a water. . . .

MÉLISANDE.

My hands do not tremble.

PÉLLÉAS.

How it shines in the sunlight! — Do not
throw it so high in the air. . . .

MÉLISANDE.

Oh! . . .

PÉLLÉAS.

It has fallen?

MÉLISANDE.

It has fallen into the water! . . .

PÉLLÉAS.

Where is it? where is it? . . .

MÉLISANDE.

I do not see it sink? . . .

PÉLLÉAS.

I think I see it shine. . . .

MÉLISANDE.

My ring?

PÉLLÉAS.

Yes, yes; down yonder. . . .

MÉLISANDE.

Oh! oh! It is so far away from us! . . .
no, no, that is not it . . . that is not it . . .
It is lost . . . lost. . . . There is nothing any
more but a great circle on the water. . . . What
shall we do? What shall we do now? . . .

6

PÉLLÉAS.

You need not be so troubled for a ring. It
is nothing. . . . We shall find it again, perhaps.
Or else we will find another. . . .

MÉLISANDE.

No, no; we shall never find it again; we
shall never find any others either. . . . And yet
I thought I had it in my hands. . . . I had
already shut my hands, and it is fallen in spite of
all. . . . I threw it too high, toward the sun. . . .

PÉLLÉAS.

Come, come, we will come back another day;
. . . come, it is time. They will come to
meet us. It was striking noon at the moment
the ring fell.

MÉLISANDE.

What shall we say to Golaud if he ask where
it is?

PÉLLÉAS.

The truth, the truth, the truth. . . .

[*Exeunt.*

SCENE II. — *An apartment in the castle.* GO-
LAUD *discovered, stretched upon his bed;*
MÉLISANDE, *by his bedside.*

GOLAUD.

Ah! ah! all goes well; it will amount to
nothing. But I cannot understand how it

came to pass. I was hunting quietly in the
forest. All at once my horse ran away, without cause. Did he see anything unusual? . . .
I had just heard the twelve strokes of noon.
At the twelfth stroke he suddenly took fright
and ran like a blind madman against a tree.
I heard no more. I do not yet know what
happened. I fell, and he must have fallen on
me. I thought I had the whole forest on my
breast ; I thought my heart was crushed. But
my heart is sound. It is nothing, apparently. . . .

MÉLISANDE.

Would you like a little water?

GOLAUD.

Thanks, thanks ; I am not thirsty.

MÉLISANDE.

Would you like another pillow? . . . There
is a little spot of blood on this.

GOLAUD.

No, no ; it is not worth while. I bled at
the mouth just now. I shall bleed again
perhaps. . . .

MÉLISANDE.

Are you quite sure? . . . You are not suffering too much?

GOLAUD.

No, no ; I have seen a good many more like
this. I was made of iron and blood. . . . These

are not the little bones of a child; do not alarm yourself. . . .

MÉLISANDE.

Close your eyes and try to sleep. I shall stay here all night. . . .

GOLAUD.

No, no; I do not wish you to tire yourself so. I do not need anything; I shall sleep like a child. . . . What is the matter, Mélisande? Why do you weep all at once? . . . .

MÉLISANDE (*bursting into tears*).

I am . . . I am ill too. . . .

GOLAUD.

Thou art ill? . . . What ails thee, then; what ails thee, Mélisande? . . .

MÉLISANDE.

I do not know. . . . I am ill here. . . . I had rather tell you to-day; my lord, my lord, I am not happy here. . . .

GOLAUD.

Why, what has happened, Mélisande? What is it? . . . And I suspecting nothing. . . . What has happened? . . . Some one has done thee harm? . . . Some one has given thee offence?

MÉLISANDE.

No, no; no one has done me the least harm. . . . It is not that. . . . It is not that. . . . But

I can live here no longer. I do not know
why. . . . I would go away, go away ! . . . I
shall die if I am left here. . . .

GOLAUD.

But something has happened? You must
be hiding something from me? . . . Tell me
the whole truth, Mélisande. . . . Is it the King?
. . . Is it my mother? . . . Is it Pélléas? . . .

MÉLISANDE.

No, no ; it is not Pélléas. It is not anybody.
. . . You could not understand me. . . .

GOLAUD.

Why should I not understand? . . . If you
tell me nothing, what will you have me do? . . .
Tell me everything and I shall understand
everything.

MÉLISANDE.

I do not know myself what it is. . . . I do not
know just what it is. . . . If I could tell you, I
would tell you. . . . It is something stronger
than I. . . .

GOLAUD.

Come ; be reasonable, Mélisande. — What
would you have me do? — You are no longer a
child. — Is it I whom you would leave?

MÉLISANDE.

Oh ! no, no ; it is not that. . . . I would go
away with you. . . . It is here that I can live no

longer. . . . I feel that I shall not live a long while. . . .

GOLAUD.

But there must be a reason nevertheless. You will be thought mad. It will be thought child's dreams. — Come, is it Pélléas, perhaps? — I think he does not often speak to you.

MÉLISANDE.

Yes, yes; he speaks to me sometimes. I think he does not like me; I have seen it in his eyes. . . . But he speaks to me when he meets me. . . .

GOLAUD.

You must not take it ill of him. He has always been so. He is a little strange. And just now he is sad; he thinks of his friend Marcellus, who is at the point of death, and whom he cannot go to see. . . . He will change, he will change, you will see; he is young. . . .

MÉLISANDE.

But it is not that . . . it is not that. . . .

GOLAUD.

What is it, then? — Can you not get used to the life one leads here? Is it too gloomy here? — It is true the castle is very old and very sombre. . . . It is very cold, and very deep. And all those who dwell in it, are already old. And the country may seem gloomy too, with all its forests, all its old forests without light. But

that may all be enlivened if we will. And
then, joy, joy, one does not have it every day;
we must take things as they come. But tell
me something; no matter what; I will do
everything you could wish. . . .

MÉLISANDE.

Yes, yes; it is true. . . . You never see the
sky here. I saw it for the first time this
morning. . . .

GOLAUD.

It is that, then, that makes you weep, my
poor Mélisande? — It is only that, then? — You
weep, not to see the sky? — Come, come, you
are no longer at the age when one may weep
for such things. . . . And then, is not the summer yonder? You will see the sky every day.
— And then, next year. . . . Come, give me
your hand; give me both your little hands.
[*He takes her hands.*] Oh! oh! these little
hands that I could crush like flowers. . . . —
Hold! where is the ring I gave you?

MÉLISANDE.

The ring?

GOLAUD.

Yes; our wedding-ring, where is it?

MÉLISANDE.

I think . . . I think it has fallen. . . .

GOLAUD.

Fallen? — Where has it fallen? — You have
not lost it?

MÉLISANDE.

No, no ; it fell . . . it must have fallen . . .
but I know where it is. . . .

GOLAUD.

Where is it?

MÉLISANDE.

You know . . . you know well . . . the
grotto by the seashore? . . .

GOLAUD.

Yes.

MÉLISANDE.

Well then, it is there. . . . It must be it
is there. . . . Yes, yes ; I remember. . . . I
went there this morning to pick up shells for
little Yniold. . . . There were some very fine
ones. . . . It slipped from my finger . . . then
the sea came in ; and I had to go out before I
had found it.

GOLAUD.

Are you sure it is there?

MÉLISANDE.

Yes, yes ; quite sure. . . . I felt it slip . . .
then, all at once, the noise of the waves. . . .

GOLAUD.

You must go look for it at once.

MÉLISANDE.

I must go look for it at once?

GOLAUD.

Yes.

MÉLISANDE.

Now? — at once? — in the dark?

GOLAUD.

Now, at once, in the dark. You must go look for it at once. I had rather have lost all I have than have lost that ring. You do not know what it is. You do not know whence it came. The sea will be very high to-night. The sea will come to take it before you. . . . Make haste. You must go look for it at once. . . .

MÉLISANDE.

I dare not. . . . I dare not go alone. . . .

GOLAUD.

Go, go with no matter whom. But you must go at once, do you understand? — Make haste; ask Pélléas to go with you.

MÉLISANDE.

Pélléas? — With Pélléas? — But Pélléas would not. . . .

GOLAUD.

Pélléas will do all you ask of him. I know Pélléas better than you do. Go, go; hurry! I shall not sleep until I have the ring.

MÉLISANDE.

Oh! oh! I am not happy! . . . I am not happy! . . .

[*Exit, weeping.*

SCENE III. — *Before a grotto.*

Enter PÉLLÉAS *and* MÉLISANDE.

PÉLLÉAS.

[*Speaking with great agitation.*] Yes; it is here; we are there. It is so dark you cannot tell the entrance of the grotto from the rest of the night. . . . There are no stars on this side. Let us wait till the moon has torn through that great cloud; it will light up the whole grotto, and then we can enter without danger. There are dangerous places, and the path is very narrow between two lakes whose bottom has not yet been found. I did not think to bring a torch or a lantern, but I think the light of the sky will be enough for us. — You have never gone into this grotto?

MÉLISANDE.

No. . . .

PÉLLÉAS.

Let us go in; let us go in. . . . You must be able to describe the place where you lost the ring, if he questions you. . . . It is very big

and very beautiful. There are stalactites that
look like plants and men. It is full of blue
darks. It has not yet been explored to the
end. There are great treasures hidden there,
it seems. You will see the remains of ancient
shipwrecks there. But you must not go far in
it without a guide. There have been some
who never have come back. I myself dare not
go forward too far. We will stop the moment
we no longer see the light of the sea or the sky.
When you strike a little light there, you would
say the vault was covered with stars like the
sky. It is bits of crystal or salt, they say, that
shine so in the rock. — Look, look, I think the
sky is going to clear. . . . Give me your hand ;
do not tremble, do not tremble so. There
is no danger ; we will stop the moment we no
longer see the light of the sea. . . . Is it the
noise of the grotto that frightens you? It is
the noise of night or the noise of silence. . . .
Do you hear the sea behind us? — It does
not seem happy to-night. . . . Ah ! look, the
light ! . . .

> [The moon lights up abundantly the entrance
> and part of the darkness of the grotto ; and
> at a certain depth are seen three old beggars
> with white hair, seated side by side, lean-
> ing upon each other and asleep against a
> bowlder.]

MÉLISANDE.

Ah !

PÉLLÉAS.

What is it?

MÉLISANDE.

There are . . . there are. . . .
        [*She points out the three beggars.*

PÉLLÉAS.

Yes, yes ; I have seen them too. . . .

MÉLISANDE.

Let us go ! . . . Let us go ! . . .

PÉLLÉAS.

Yes . . . it is three old poor men fallen asleep.
. . . There is a famine in the country. . . .
Why have they come to sleep here ? . . .

MÉLISANDE.

Let us go ! . . . Come, come. . . . Let
us go ! . . .

PÉLLÉAS.

Take care ; do not speak so loud. . . . Let
us not wake them. . . . They are still sleeping
heavily. . . . Come.

MÉLISANDE.

Leave me, leave me ; I prefer to walk
alone. . . .

PÉLLÉAS.

We will come back another day. . . . [*Exeunt.*

SCENE IV. — *An apartment in the castle.*
ARKËL *and* PÉLLÉAS *discovered.*

ARKËL.

You see that everything retains you here just
now and forbids you this useless journey. We
have concealed your father's condition from
you until now ; but it is perhaps hopeless ; and
that alone should suffice to stop you on the
threshold. But there are so many other rea-
sons. . . . And it is not in the day when our
enemies awake, and when the people are dying
of hunger and murmur about us, that you have
the right to desert us. And why this journey?
Marcellus is dead ; and life has graver duties
than the visit to a tomb. You are weary, you
say, of your inactive life ; but activity and duty
are not found on the highways. They must be
waited for upon the threshold, and let in as they
go by ; and they go by every day. You have
never seen them? I hardly see them any more
myself ; but I will teach you to see them, and I
will point them out to you the day when you
would make them a sign. Nevertheless, listen
to me ; if you believe it is from the depths of
your life this journey is exacted, I do not for-
bid your undertaking it, for you must know
better than I the events you must offer to your
being or your fate. I shall ask you only to
wait until we know what must take place ere
long. . . .

PÉLLÉAS.

How long must I wait?

ARKËL.

A few weeks; perhaps a few days. . . .

PÉLLÉAS.

I will wait. . . .

ACT THIRD.

SCENE I. — *An apartment in the castle.* PÉL-
LÉAS *and* MÉLISANDE *discovered.* MÉLISANDE
plies her distaff at the back of the room.

PÉLLÉAS.

Yniold does not come back; where has he
gone?

MÉLISANDE.

He had heard something in the corridor; he
has gone to see what it is.

PÉLLÉAS.

Mélisande. . . .

MÉLISANDE.

What is it?

PÉLLÉAS.

. . . Can you see still to work there? . . .

MÉLISANDE.

I work as well in the dark. . . .

PÉLLÉAS.

I think everybody is already asleep in the
castle. Golaud does not come back from the
chase. It is late, nevertheless. . . . He no
longer suffers from his fall? . . .

MÉLISANDE.

He said he no longer suffered from it.

PÉLLÉAS.

He must be more prudent; his body is no longer as supple as at twenty years. . . . I see the stars through the window and the light of the moon on the trees. It is late; he will not come back now. [*Knocking at the door.*] Who is there? . . . Come in! . . .

Little YNIOLD *opens the door and enters the room.*

It was you knocking so? . . . That is not the way to knock at doors. It is as if a misfortune had arrived; look, you have frightened little mother.

LITTLE YNIOLD.

I only knocked a tiny little bit.

PÉLLÉAS.

It is late; little father will not come back to-night; it is time for you to go to bed.

LITTLE YNIOLD.

I shall not go to bed before you do.

PÉLLÉAS.

What? . . . What is that you are saying?

LITTLE YNIOLD.

I say . . . not before you . . . not before
you . . .

> [*Bursts into sobs and takes refuge by*
> MÉLISANDE.]

MÉLISANDE.

What is it, Yniold? . . . What is it? . . .
why do you weep all at once?

YNIOLD (*sobbing*).

Because . . . oh! oh! because . . .

MÉLISANDE.

Because what? . . . Because what? . . .
Tell me . . .

YNIOLD.

Little mother . . . little mother . . . you
are going away. . . .

MÉLISANDE.

But what has taken hold of you, Yniold? . . .
I have never dreamed of going away. . . .

YNIOLD.

Yes, you have; yes, you have; little father
has gone away. . . . Little father does not come
back, and you are going to go away too. . . . I
have seen it . . . I have seen it. . . .

MÉLISANDE.

But there has never been any idea of that,
Yniold. . . . Why, what makes you think that
I would go away? . . .

YNIOLD.

I have seen it . . . I have seen it. . . . You
have said things to uncle that I could not
hear . . .

PÉLLÉAS.

He is sleepy. . . . He has been dreaming. . . .
Come here, Yniold; asleep already? . . .
Come and look out at the window; the swans
are fighting with the dogs. . . .

YNIOLD (*at the window*).

Oh! oh! they are chasing the dogs! . . .
They are chasing them! . . . Oh! oh! the
water! . . . the wings! . . the wings! . . .
they are afraid. . . .

PÉLLÉAS (*coming back by* MÉLISANDE).

He is sleepy; he is struggling against sleep;
his eyes were closing. . . .

MÉLISANDE (*singing softly as she spins*).

Saint Daniel and Saint Michaël. . . .
Saint Michaël and Saint Raphaël. . . .

YNIOLD (*at the window*).

Oh! oh! little mother! . . .

MÉLISANDE (*rising abruptly*).

What is it, Yniold? . . . What is it? . . .

YNIOLD.

I saw something at the window? . . .
[PÉLLÉAS *and* MÉLISANDE *run to the window.*

PÉLLÉAS.

What is there at the window? . . . What
have you seen? . . .

YNIOLD.

Oh! oh! I saw something! . . .

PÉLLÉAS.

But there is nothing.   I see nothing. . . .

MÉLISANDE.

Nor I. . . .

PÉLLÉAS.

Where did you see something? Which
way? . . .

YNIOLD.

Down there, down there! . . . It is no
longer there. . . .

PÉLLÉAS.

He does not know what he is saying.   He
must have seen the light of the moon on the
forest.   There are often strange reflections, . . .
or else something must have passed on the

highway . . . or in his sleep. For see, see, I
believe he is quite asleep. . . .

YNIOLD (*at the window*).

Little father is there ! little father is there !

PÉLLÉAS (*going to the window*).

He is right ; Golaud is coming into the
courtyard. . . .

YNIOLD.

Little father ! . . . little father ! . . . I am
going to meet him ! . . .

[*Exit, running. — A silence.*

PÉLLÉAS.

They are coming up the stair. . . .

Enter GOLAUD *and little* YNIOLD *with a lamp.*

GOLAUD.

You are still waiting in the dark ?

YNIOLD.

I have brought a light, little mother, a big
light ! . . . [*He lifts the lamp and looks at*
MÉLISANDE.] You have been weeping, little
mother ? . . . You have been weeping ? . . .
[*He lifts the lamp toward* PÉLLÉAS *and looks
in turn at him.*] You too, you too, you have
been weeping ? . . . Little father, look, little
father ; they have both been weeping. . . .

GOLAUD.

Do not hold the light under their eyes
so. . . .

SCENE II. — *One of the towers of the castle.* —
*A watchman's round passes under a window
in the tower.*

MÉLISANDE (*at the window, combing her
unbound hair*).

My long locks fall foaming
    To the threshold of the tower, —
My locks await your coming
    All along the tower,
And all the long, long hour,
And all the long, long hour.

*Saint Daniel and Saint Michaël,
Saint Michaël and Saint Raphaël.*

I was born on a Sunday,
    A Sunday at high noon. . . .

Enter PÉLLÉAS *by the watchman's round.*

PÉLLÉAS.

Holà! Holà! ho! . . .

MÉLISANDE.

Who is there?

PÉLLÉAS.

I, I, and I! . . . What art thou doing there
at the window, singing like a bird that is not
native here?

MÉLISANDE.

I am doing my hair for the night. . . .

PÉLLÉAS.

Is it that I see upon the wall? . . . I
thought you had some light. . . .

MÉLISANDE.

I have opened the window; it is too hot in
the tower. . . . It is beautiful to-night. . . .

PÉLLÉAS.

There are innumerable stars; I have never
seen so many as to-night; . . . but the moon
is still upon the sea. . . . Do not stay in the
shadow, Mélisande; lean forward a little till I
see your unbound hair. . . .

MÉLISANDE.

I am frightful so. . . .
                    [*She leans out at the window.*

PÉLLÉAS.

Oh! oh! Mélisande! . . . oh, thou art
beautiful! . . . thou art beautiful so! . . .
Lean out! lean out! . . . Let me come nearer
thee . . .

MÉLISANDE.

I cannot come nearer thee. . . . I am leaning out as far as I can. . . .

PÉLLÉAS.

I cannot come up higher; . . . give me at least thy hand to-night . . . before I go away. . . . I leave to-morrow. . . .

MÉLISANDE.

No, no, no ! . . .

PÉLLÉAS.

Yes, yes, yes; I leave, I shall leave to-morrow. . . . Give me thy hand, thy hand, thy little hand upon my lips. . . .

MÉLISANDE.

I give thee not my hand if thou wilt leave. . . .

PÉLLÉAS.

Give, give, give ! . . .

MÉLISANDE.

Thou wilt not leave ? . . .

PÉLLÉAS.

I will wait; I will wait. . . .

MÉLISANDE.

I see a rose in the shadows. . . .

PÉLLÉAS.

Where ? . . . I see only the boughs of the willow hanging over the wall. . . .

MÉLISANDE.

Further down, further down, in the garden; further down, in the sombre green. . . .

PÉLLÉAS.

It is not a rose. . . . I will go see by and by, but give me thy hand first; first thy hand. . . .

MÉLISANDE.

There, there; . . . I cannot lean out further. . . .

PÉLLÉAS.

I cannot reach thy hand with my lips. . . .

MÉLISANDE.

I cannot lean out further. . . . I am on the point of falling. . . . — Oh! oh! my hair is falling down the tower! . . .

> [*Her tresses fall suddenly over her head, as she is leaning out so, and stream over* PÉLLÉAS.]

PÉLLÉAS.

Oh! oh! what is it? . . . Thy hair, thy hair is falling down to me! . . . All thy locks, Mélisande, all thy locks have fallen down the tower! . . . I hold them in my hands; I hold them in my mouth. . . . I hold them in my arms; I put them about my neck. . . . I will not open my hands again to-night. . . .

MÉLISANDE.

Let me go ! let me go ! . . . Thou wilt make me fall ! . . .

PÉLLÉAS.

No, no, no ; . . . I have never seen such hair as thine, Mélisande ! . . . See, see, see ; it comes from so high and yet it floods me to the heart ! . . . And yet it floods me to the knees ! . . . And it is sweet, sweet as if it fell from heaven ! . . . I see the sky no longer through thy locks. Thou seest, thou seest ? . . . I can no longer hold them with both hands ; there are some on the boughs of the willow. . . . They are alive like birds in my hands, . . . and they love me, they love me more than thou ! . . .

MÉLISANDE.

Let me go ; let me go ! . . . Some one might come. . . .

PÉLLÉAS.

No, no, no ; I shall not set thee free to-night. . . . Thou art my prisoner to-night ; all night, all night ! . . .

MÉLISANDE.

Pélléas ! Pélléas ! . . .

PÉLLÉAS.

I tie them, I tie them to the willow boughs. . . . Thou shalt not go away now ; . . . thou shalt not go away now. . . . Look, look, I am kissing thy hair. . . . I suffer no more in the midst of thy hair. . . . Hearest thou my kisses along thy hair? . . . They mount along thy hair. . . . Each hair must bring thee some. . . . Thou seest, thou seest, I can open my hands. . . . My hands are free, and thou canst not leave me now. . . .

MÉLISANDE.

Oh! oh! thou hurtest me. . . . [*Doves come out of the tower and fly about them in the night.*] — What is that, Pélléas? — What is it flying about me?

PÉLLÉAS.

It is the doves coming out of the tower. . . . I have frightened them; they are flying away. . . .

MÉLISANDE.

It is my doves, Pélléas. — Let us go away, let me go; they will not come back again. . . .

PÉLLÉAS.

Why will they not come back again?

MÉLISANDE.

They will be lost in the dark. . . . Let me go; let me lift my head. . . . I hear a noise of footsteps. . . . Let me go! — It is Golaud! . . . I believe it is Golaud! . . . He has heard us. . . .

PÉLLÉAS.

Wait! Wait! . . . Thy hair is about the boughs. . . . It is caught there in the darkness. . . . Wait, wait! . . . It is dark. . . .

Enter GOLAUD, *by the watchman's round.*

GOLAUD.

What do you here?

PÉLLÉAS.

What do I here? . . . I . . .

GOLAUD.

You are children. . . . Mélisande, do not lean out so at the window; you will fall. . . . Do you not know it is late? — It is nearly midnight. — Do not play so in the darkness. — You are children. . . . [*Laughing nervously.*] What children! . . . What children! . . .

[*Exit, with* PÉLLÉAS.

SCENE III. — *The vaults of the castle.*

Enter GOLAUD *and* PÉLLÉAS.

GOLAUD.

Take care; this way, this way. — You have never penetrated into these vaults?

PÉLLÉAS.

Yes; once, of old; but it was long ago. . . .

GOLAUD.

They are prodigious great; it is a succession of enormous crypts that end, God knows where. The whole castle is builded on these crypts. Do you smell the deathly odor that reigns here? — That is what I wished to show you. In my opinion, it comes from the little underground lake I am going to have you see. Take care; walk before me, in the light of my lantern. I will warn you when we are there. [*They continue to walk in silence.*] Hey! hey! Pélléas! stop! stop! — [*He seizes him by the arm.*] For God's sake! . . . Do you not see? — One step more, and you had been in the gulf! . . .

PÉLLÉAS.

But I did not see it! . . . The lantern no longer lighted me. . . .

GOLAUD.

I made a misstep, . . . but if I had not held you by the arm . . . Well, this is the stagnant water that I spoke of to you. . . . Do you perceive the smell of death that rises? — Let us go to the end of this overhanging rock, and do you lean over a little. It will strike you in the face.

PÉLLÉAS.

I smell it already; . . . you would say a smell of the tomb.

GOLAUD.

Further, further. . . . It is this that on cer-
tain days has poisoned the castle. The King
will not believe it comes from here. — The
crypt should be walled up in which this standing water is found. It is time, besides, to
examine these vaults a little. Have you noticed
those lizards on the walls and pillars of the
vaults? — There is a labor hidden here you
would not suspect; and the whole castle will be
swallowed up one of these nights, if it is not
looked out for. But what will you have? nobody likes to come down this far. . . . There
are strange lizards in many of the walls. . . .
Oh! here . . . do you perceive the smell of
death that rises?

PÉLLÉAS.

Yes; there is a smell of death rising about
us. . . .

GOLAUD.

Lean over; have no fear. . . . I will hold
you . . . give me . . . no, no, not your hand
. . . it might slip . . . your arm, your arm!
. . . Do you see the gulf? [*Moved.*] — Pélléas? Pélléas? . . .

PÉLLÉAS.

Yes; I think I see the bottom of the gulf.
. . . Is it the light that trembles so? . . . You
. . . [*He straightens up, turns, and looks at*
GOLAUD.]

GOLAUD (*with a trembling voice*).

Yes; it is the lantern. . . . See, I shook it to lighten the walls. . . .

PÉLLÉAS.

I stifle here; . . . let us go out. . . .

GOLAUD.

Yes; let us go out. . . .

[*Exeunt in silence.*

SCENE IV. — *A terrace at the exit of the vaults. Enter* GOLAUD *and* PÉLLÉAS.

PÉLLÉAS.

Ah! I breathe at last! . . . I thought, one moment, I was going to be ill in those enormous crypts; I was on the point of falling. . . . There is a damp air there, heavy as a leaden dew, and darkness thick as a poisoned paste. . . . And now, all the air of all the sea! . . . There is a fresh wind, see; fresh as a leaf that has just opened, over the little green waves. . . . Hold! the flowers have just been watered at the foot of the terrace, and the smell of the verdure and the wet roses comes up to us. . . . It must be nearly noon; they are already in the shadow of the tower. . . . It is noon; I hear the bells ringing, and the children are going down to the beach to bathe. . . . I did not

know that we had stayed so long in the
caverns. . . .

GOLAUD.

We went down towards eleven o'clock. . . .

PÉLLÉAS.

Earlier; it must have been earlier; I heard
it strike half-past ten.

GOLAUD.

Half-past ten or a quarter to eleven. . . .

PÉLLÉAS.

They have opened all the windows of the
castle. It will be unusually hot this afternoon.
. . . Look, there is mother with Mélisande at a
window of the tower. . . .

GOLAUD.

Yes; they have taken refuge on the shady
side. — Speaking of Mélisande, I heard what
passed and what was said last night. I am quite
aware all that is but child's play; but it need
not be repeated. Mélisande is very young and
very impressionable; and she must be treated
the more circumspectly that she is perhaps with
child at this moment. . . . She is very delicate,
hardly woman; and the least emotion might
bring on a mishap. It is not the first time I
have noticed there might be something between
you. . . . You are older than she; it will suffice
to have told you. . . . Avoid her as much as

possible; without affectation moreover; without affectation. . . . — What is it I see yonder on the highway toward the forest? . . .

PÉLLÉAS.

Some herds they are leading to the city. . . .

GOLAUD.

They cry like lost children; you would say they smelt the butcher already.— It will be time for dinner.— What a fine day! What a capital day for the harvest! . . .

[*Exeunt.*

SCENE V. — *Before the castle.*

Enter GOLAUD *and little* YNIOLD.

GOLAUD.

Come, we are going to sit down here, Yniold; sit on my knee; we shall see from here what passes in the forest. I do not see you any more at all now. You abandon me too; you are always at little mother's. . . . Why, we are sitting just under little mother's windows. — Perhaps she is saying her evening prayer at this moment. . . . But tell me, Yniold, she is often with your uncle Pélléas, is n't she?

YNIOLD.

Yes, yes; always, little father; when you are not there, little father. . . .

GOLAUD.

Ah! — look; some one is going by with a lantern in the garden. — But I have been told they did not like each other. . . . It seems they often quarrel; . . . no? Is it true?

YNIOLD.

Yes, yes; it is true.

GOLAUD.

Yes? — Ah! ah! — But what do they quarrel about?

YNIOLD.

About the door.

GOLAUD.

What? about the door? — What are you talking about? — No, come, explain yourself; why do they quarrel about the door?

YNIOLD.

Because it won't stay open.

GOLAUD.

Who wants it to stay open? — Come, why do they quarrel?

YNIOLD.

I don't know, little father; about the light.

GOLAUD.

I am not talking to you about the light; we will talk of that by and by. I am talking to

8

you about the door. Answer what I ask you ;
you must learn to talk ; it is time. . . . Do
not put your hand in your mouth so ; . . .
come. . . .

YNIOLD.

Little father ! little father ! . . . I won't do
it any more. . . . [*He cries.*]

GOLAUD.

Come ; what are you crying for now? What
has happened ?

YNIOLD.

Oh ! oh ! little father, you hurt me. . . .

GOLAUD.

I hurt you? — Where did I hurt you? I did
not mean to. . . .

YNIOLD.

Here, here ; on my little arm. . . .

GOLAUD.

I did not mean to ; come, don't cry any
more, and I will give you something to-morrow.

YNIOLD.

What, little father ?

GOLAUD.

A quiver and some arrows ; but tell me what
you know about the door.

YNIOLD.

Big arrows?

GOLAUD.

Yes, yes; very big arrows. — But why don't they want the door to be open? — Come, answer me sometime! — no, no; do not open your mouth to cry. I am not angry. We are going to have a quiet talk, like Pélléas and little mother when they are together. What do they talk about when they are together?

YNIOLD.

Pélléas and little mother?

GOLAUD.

Yes; what do they talk about?

YNIOLD.

About me; always about me.

GOLAUD.

And what do they say about you?

YNIOLD.

They say I am going to be very big.

GOLAUD.

Oh, plague of my life! . . . I am here like a blind man searching for his treasure at the bottom of the ocean! . . . I am here like a new-born child lost in the forest, and you . . . Come, come, Yniold, I was wandering; we are

going to talk seriously. Do Pélléas and little
mother never speak of me when I am not
there? . . .

YNIOLD.

Yes, yes, little father; they are always speaking of you.

GOLAUD.

Ah! . . . And what do they say of me?

YNIOLD.

They say I shall grow as big as you are.

GOLAUD.

You are always by them?

YNIOLD.

Yes, yes, always, always, little father.

GOLAUD.

They never tell you to go play somewhere
else?

YNIOLD.

No, little father; they are afraid when I am
not there.

GOLAUD.

They are afraid? . . . What makes you
think they are afraid?

YNIOLD.

Little mother always says, "Don't go away;
don't go away!" . . . They are unhappy, but
they laugh. . . .

GOLAUD.

But that does not prove they are afraid.

YNIOLD.

Yes, yes, little father; she is afraid. . . .

GOLAUD.

Why do you say she is afraid?

YNIOLD.

They always weep in the dark.

GOLAUD.

Ah! ah! . . .

YNIOLD.

That makes one weep too.

GOLAUD.

Yes, yes! . . .

YNIOLD.

She is pale, little father.

GOLAUD.

Ah! ah! . . . patience, my God, patience! . . .

YNIOLD.

What, little father?

GOLAUD.

Nothing, nothing, my child. — I saw a wolf go by in the forest. — Then they get on well together? — I am glad to learn they are on

good terms. — They kiss each other sometimes?
— No? . . .

YNIOLD.

Kiss each other, little father? — No, no, —
ah ! yes, little father, yes, yes ; once . . . once
when it rained. . . .

GOLAUD.

They kissed? — But how, how did they kiss?

YNIOLD.

So, little father, so ! . . . [*He gives him a
kiss on the mouth, laughing.*] Ah ! ah ! your
beard, little father ! . . . It pricks ! it pricks !
it pricks ! It is getting all gray, little father,
and your hair, too ; all gray, all gray, all gray.
. . . [*The window under which they are sitting
is lighted up at this moment, and the light falls
upon them.*] Ah ! ah ! little mother has lit her
lamp. It is light, little father ; it is light. . . .

GOLAUD.

Yes ; it is beginning to be light. . . .

YNIOLD.

Let us go there too, little father ; let us go
there too. . . .

GOLAUD.

Where do you want to go?

YNIOLD.

Where it is light, little father.

GOLAUD.

No, no, my child; let us stay in the dark a little longer. . . . One cannot tell, one cannot tell yet. . . . Do you see those poor people down there trying to kindle a little fire in the forest? — It has rained. And over there, do you see the old gardener trying to lift that tree the wind has blown down across the road? — He cannot; the tree is too big; the tree is too heavy, and it will lie where it fell. All that cannot be helped. . . . I think Pélléas is mad. . . .

YNIOLD.

No, little father, he is not mad; he is very good.

GOLAUD.

Do you want to see little mother?

YNIOLD.

Yes, yes; I want to see her!

GOLAUD.

Don't make any noise; I am going to hoist you up to the window. It is too high for me, for all I am so big. . . . [*He lifts the child.*] Do not make the least noise; little mother would be terribly afraid. . . . Do you see her? — Is she in the room?

YNIOLD.

Yes. . . . Oh, how light it is!

GOLAUD.

She is alone?

YNIOLD.

Yes; . . . no, no ; Uncle Pélléas is there, too.

GOLAUD.

He— . . . !

YNIOLD.

Ah ! ah ! little father ! you have hurt me ! . . .

GOLAUD.

It is nothing; be still; I will not do it any more ; look, look, Yniold ! . . . I stumbled; speak lower. What are they doing?—

YNIOLD.

They are not doing anything, little father; they are waiting for something.

GOLAUD.

Are they near each other?

YNIOLD.

No, little father.

GOLAUD.

And . . . and the bed? are they near the bed?

YNIOLD.

The bed, little father?— I can't see the bed.

GOLAUD.

Lower, lower; they will hear you. Are they speaking?

YNIOLD.

No, little father ; they do not speak.

GOLAUD.

But what are they doing?—They must be doing something. . . .

YNIOLD.

They are looking at the light.

GOLAUD.

Both?

YNIOLD.

Yes, little father.

GOLAUD.

They do not say anything?

YNIOLD.

No, little father ; they do not close their eyes.

GOLAUD.

They do not come near each other?

YNIOLD.

No, little father ; they do not stir.

GOLAUD.

They are sitting down?

YNIOLD.

No, little father ; they are standing upright against the wall.

GOLAUD.

They make no gestures? — They do not look at each other? — They make no signs? . . .

YNIOLD.

No, little father. — Oh! oh! little father; they never close their eyes. . . . I am terribly afraid. . . .

GOLAUD.

Be still. They do not stir yet?

YNIOLD.

No, little father. — I am afraid, little father; let me come down! . . .

GOLAUD.

Why, what are you afraid of? — Look! look! . . .

YNIOLD.

I dare not look any more, little father! . . . Let me come down! . . .

GOLAUD.

Look! look! . . .

YNIOLD.

Oh! oh! I am going to cry, little father! — Let me come down! let me come down! . . .

GOLAUD.

Come; we will go see what has happened.

[*Exeunt.*

ACT FOURTH.

SCENE I. — *A corridor in the castle.*

Enter PÉLLÉAS *and* MÉLISANDE, *meeting.*

PÉLLÉAS.

Where goest thou? I must speak to thee
to-night. Shall I see thee?

MÉLISANDE.

Yes.

PÉLLÉAS.

I have just left my father's room. He is
getting better. The physician has told us he is
saved. . . . And yet this morning I had a pre-
sentiment this day would end ill. I have had
a rumor of misfortune in my ears for some time.
. . . Then, all at once there was a great change;
to-day it is no longer anything but a question
of time. All the windows in his room have
been thrown open. He speaks; he seems
happy. He does not speak yet like an ordinary man, but already his ideas no longer all
come from the other world. . . . He recognized me. He took my hand and said with
that strange air he has had since he fell sick:
"Is it thou, Pélléas? Why, why, I had not
noticed it before, but thou hast the grave and

friendly look of those who will not live long.
. . . You must travel; you must travel. . . ."
It is strange; I shall obey him. . . . My
mother listened to him and wept for joy. —
Hast thou not been aware of it? — The whole
house seems already to revive, you hear breathing, you hear speaking, you hear walking.
. . . Listen; I hear some one speaking behind
that door. Quick, quick! answer quickly!
where shall I see thee?

MÉLISANDE.

Where wouldst thou?

PÉLLÉAS.

In the park; near "Blind Man's Spring."
— Wilt thou? — Wilt thou come?

MÉLISANDE.

Yes.

PÉLLÉAS.

It will be the last night; — I am going to
travel, as my father said. Thou wilt not see me
more. . . .

MÉLISANDE.

Do not say that, Pélléas. . . . I shall see
thee always; I shall look upon thee always. . . .

PÉLLÉAS.

Thou wilt look in vain. . . . I shall be so
far away thou couldst no longer see me. . . .
I shall try to go very far away. . . . I am full

of joy, and you would say I had all the weight
of heaven and earth on my body to-day. . . .

MÉLISANDE.

What has happened, Pélléas? — I no longer
understand what you say. . . .

PÉLLÉAS.

Go, go; let us separate.   I hear some one
speaking behind that door. . . . It is the
strangers who came to the castle this morning.
. . . They are going out. . . . Let us go; it is
the strangers. . . .   [*Exeunt severally.*

SCENE II. — *An apartment in the castle.*
ARKËL *and* MÉLISANDE *discovered.*

ARKËL.

Now that Pélléas's father is saved, and sick-
ness, the old handmaid of Death, has left the
castle, a little joy and a little sunlight will at last
come into the house again. . . . It was time !
— For, since thy coming, we have only lived
here whispering about a closed room. . . . And
truly I have pitied thee, Mélisande. . . . Thou
camest here all joyous, like a child seeking a gala-day, and at the moment thou en-
teredst in the vestibule I saw thy face change,
and probably thy soul, as the face changes
in spite of us when we enter at noon into
a grotto too gloomy and too cold. . . . And

since, — since, on account of all that, I have often no longer understood thee. . . . I observed thee, thou wert there, listless perhaps, but with the strange, astray look of one awaiting ever a great trouble, in the sunlight, in a beautiful garden. . . . I cannot explain. . . . But I was sad to see thee so ; for thou art too young and too beautiful to live already day and night under the breath of death. . . . But now all that will change. At my age, — and there perhaps is the surest fruit of my life, — at my age I have gained I know not what faith in the fidelity of events, and I have always seen that every young and beautiful being creates about itself young, beautiful, and happy events. . . . And it is thou who wilt now open the door for the new era I have glimpses of. . . . Come here ; why dost thou stay there without answering and without lifting thine eyes? — I have kissed thee but once only hitherto, — the day of thy coming ; and yet old men need sometimes to touch with their lips a woman's forehead or a child's cheek, to believe still in the freshness of life and avert awhile the menaces. . . . Art thou afraid of my old lips? How I have pitied thee these months ! . . .

MÉLISANDE.

Grandfather, I have not been unhappy. . . .

ARKËL.

Perhaps you were of those who are unhappy without knowing it, . . . and they are the most

unhappy. . . . Let me look at thee, so, quite
near, a moment; . . . we have such need of
beauty beside Death. . . .

Enter GOLAUD.

GOLAUD.

Pélléas leaves to-night.

ARKËL.

Thou hast blood on thy forehead. — What
hast thou done?

GOLAUD.

Nothing, nothing. . . . I have passed through
a hedge of thorns.

MÉLISANDE.

Bend down your head a little, my lord. . . .
I will wipe your forehead. . . .

GOLAUD (*repulsing her*).

I will not that you touch me, do you understand?   Go, go! — I am not speaking to you.
— Where is my sword? — I came to seek my
sword. . . .

MÉLISANDE.

Here; on the praying-stool.

GOLAUD.

Bring it.   [*To* ARKËL.] — They have just
found another peasant dead of hunger, along by
the sea.   You would say they all meant to die

under our eyes. — [*To* MÉLISANDE.] Well, my
sword? — Why do you tremble so? — I am not
going to kill you. I would simply examine the
blade. I do not employ the sword for these
uses. Why do you examine me like a beggar?
— I do not come to ask alms of you. You
hope to see something in my eyes without my
seeing anything in yours? — Do you think I
may know something? — [*To* ARKËL.] — Do
you see those great eyes? — It is as if they
were proud of their richness. . . .

ARKËL.

I see there only a great innocence. . . .

GOLAUD.

A great innocence! . . . They are greater
than innocence! . . . They are purer than the
eyes of a lamb. . . . They would give God les-
sons in innocence! A great innocence! Listen:
I am so near them I feel the freshness of their
lashes when they wink; and yet I am less far
away from the great secrets of the other world
than from the smallest secret of those eyes!
. . . A great innocence! . . . More than innocence! You would say the angels of heaven
celebrated there an eternal baptism! . . . I
know those eyes! I have seen them at their
work! Close them! close them! or I shall
close them for a long while! . . . — Do not put
your right hand to your throat so; I am saying
a very simple thing. . . . I have no under-
thought. . . . If I had an under-thought, why

should I not say it? Ah! ah!—do not at-
tempt to flee!—Here!—Give me that hand!
—Ah! your hands are too hot. . . . Go away!
Your flesh disgusts me! . . . Here!—There
is no more question of fleeing now!—[*He
seizes her by the hair.*]—You shall follow me on
your knees!—On your knees!—On your knees
before me!—Ah! ah! your long hair serves
some purpose at last! . . . Right, . . . left!—
Left, . . . right!—Absalom! Absalom.—Forward! back! To the ground! to the ground!
. . . You see, you see; I laugh already like an
old man. . . .

ARKËL (*running up*).

Golaud! . . .

GOLAUD (*affecting a sudden calm*).

You will do as you may please, look you.—
I attach no importance to that.—I am too old;
and, besides, I am not a spy. I shall await
chance; and then . . . Oh! then! . . . simply
because it is the custom; simply because it is the
custom. . . .   [*Exit.*

ARKËL.

What ails him?—He is drunk?

MÉLISANDE (*in tears*).

No, no; he does not love me any more. . . .
I am not happy! . . . I am not happy! . . .

ARKËL.

If I were God, I would have pity on men's
hearts. . . .

9

SCENE III. — *A terrace of the castle.* *Little*
YNIOLD *discovered, trying to lift a bowlder.*

LITTLE YNIOLD.

Oh, this stone is heavy ! . . . It is heavier
than I am. . . . It is heavier than everybody.
. . . It is heavier than everything that ever
happened. . . . I can see my golden ball
between the rock and this naughty stone, and I
cannot reach it. . . . My little arm is not long
enough, . . . and this stone won't be lifted.
. . . I can't lift it, . . . and nobody could lift
it. . . . It is heavier than the whole house ; . . .
you would think it had roots in the earth. . . .
[*The bleatings of a flock heard far away.*] —
Oh ! oh ! I hear the sheep crying. . . . [*He
goes to look, at the edge of the terrace.*] Why !
there is no more sun. . . . They are coming
. . . the little sheep . . . they are coming.
. . . There is a lot of them ! . . . There is a
lot of them ! . . . They are afraid of the dark.
. . . They crowd together ! they crowd together ! . . . They can hardly walk any more.
. . . They are crying ! they are crying ! and
they go quick ! . . . They go quick ! . . .
They are already at the great crossroads. Ah !
ah ! They don't know where they ought to go
any more. . . . They don't cry any more. . . .
They wait. . . . Some of them want to go to
the right. . . . They all want to go to the right.
. . . They cannot ! . . . The shepherd is throw-
ing earth at them. . . . Ah ! ah ! They are
going to pass by here. . . . They obey ! They

obey! They are going to pass under the terrace. . . . They are going to pass under the
rocks. . . . I am going to see them near by.
. . . Oh! oh! what a lot of them! . . . What
a lot of them! . . . The whole road is full of
them. . . . They all keep still now. . . Shepherd! shepherd! why don't they speak any
more?

THE SHEPHERD (*who is out of sight*).

Because it is no longer the road to the
stable. . . .

YNIOLD.

Where are they going?—Shepherd! shepherd!—where are they going?—He doesn't
hear me any more. They are too far away
already. . . . They go quick. . . . They are
not making a noise any more. . . . It is no
longer the road to the stable. . . . Where are
they going to sleep to-night?—Oh! oh!—It
is too dark. . . . I am going to tell something to somebody. . . .   [*Exit.*

SCENE IV.—*A fountain in the park.*

Enter PÉLLÉAS.

PÉLLÉAS.

It is the last evening . . . the last evening.
It must all end. I have played like a child
about a thing I did not guess. . . . I have

played a-dream about the snares of fate. . . .
Who has awakened me all at once? I shall flee,
crying out for joy and woe like a blind man
fleeing from his burning house. . . . I am going
to tell her I shall flee. . . . My father is out
of danger; and I have no more reason to lie to
myself. . . . It is late; she does not come.
. . . I should do better to go away without
seeing her again. . . . I must look well at her
this time. . . . There are some things that I
no longer recall. . . . It seems at times as if
I had not seen her for a hundred years. . . .
And I have not yet looked upon her look. . . .
There remains nought to me if I go away thus.
And all those memories . . . it is as if I were
to take away a little water in a muslin bag. . . .
I must see her one last time, to the bottom of
her heart. . . . I must tell her all that I have
never told her.

Enter MÉLISANDE.

MÉLISANDE.

Pélléas !

PÉLLÉAS.

Mélisande ! — Is it thou, Mélisande?

MÉLISANDE.

Yes.

PÉLLÉAS.

Come hither; do not stay at the edge of the
moonlight. — Come hither. We have so many
things to tell each other. . . . Come hither in
the shadow of the linden.

MÉLISANDE.

Let me stay in the light. . . .

PÉLLÉAS.

We might be seen from the windows of the tower. Come hither; here, we have nothing to fear. — Take care; we might be seen. . . .

MÉLISANDE.

I wish to be seen. . . .

PÉLLÉAS.

Why, what doth ail thee? — Thou wert able to come out without being seen?

MÉLISANDE.

Yes; your brother slept. . . .

PÉLLÉAS.

It is late. — In an hour they will close the gates. We must be careful. Why art thou come so late?

MÉLISANDE.

Your brother had a bad dream. And then my gown was caught on the nails of the gate. See, it is torn. I lost all this time, and ran. . . .

PÉLLÉAS.

My poor Mélisande! . . . I should almost be afraid to touch thee. . . . Thou art still out of breath, like a hunted bird. . . . It is for me,

for me, thou doest all that? . . . I hear thy
heart beat as if it were mine. . . . Come hither
. . . nearer, nearer me. . . .

MÉLISANDE.

Why do you laugh?

PÉLLÉAS.

I do not laugh; — or else I laugh for joy,
unwittingly. . . . It were a weeping matter,
rather. . . .

MÉLISANDE.

We have come here before. . . . I recol-
lect. . . .

PÉLLÉAS.

Yes . . . yes. . . . Long months ago. — I
knew not then. . . . Knowest thou why I asked
thee to come here to-night?

MÉLISANDE.

No.

PÉLLÉAS.

It is perhaps the last time I shall see thee.
. . . I must go away forever. . . .

MÉLISANDE.

Why sayest thou always thou wilt go
away? . . .

PÉLLÉAS.

I must tell thee what thou knowest already? —
Thou knowest not what I am going to tell thee?

MÉLISANDE.

Why, no ; why, no ; I know nothing — . . .

PÉLLÉAS.

Thou knowest not why I must go afar. . . .
Thou knowest not it is because . . . [*He
kisses her abruptly.*]   I love thee. . . .

MÉLISANDE (*in a low voice*).

I love thee too. . . .

PÉLLÉAS.

Oh ! oh ! What saidst thou, Mélisande ? . . .
I hardly heard it ! . . . Thou sayest that in a
voice coming from the end of the world ! . . .
I hardly heard thee. . . . Thou lovest me ? —
Thou lovest me too ? . . . Since when lovest
thou me ? . . .

MÉLISANDE.

Since always. . . . Since I saw thee. . . .

PÉLLÉAS.

Oh, how thou sayest that ! . . . Thy voice
seems to have blown across the sea in spring !
. . . I have never heard it until now ; . . . one
would say it had rained on my heart ! . . .
Thou sayest that so frankly ! . . . Like an
angel questioned ! . . . I cannot believe it,
Mélisande ! . . . Why shouldst thou love me ?
— Nay, why dost thou love me ? — Is what thou
sayest true ? — Thou dost not mock me ? —

Thou dost not lie a little, to make me
smile? . . .

MÉLISANDE.

No; I never lie; I lie but to thy
brother. . . .

PÉLLÉAS.

Oh, how thou sayest that! . . . Thy voice!
thy voice! . . . It is cooler and more frank
than the water is! . . . It is like pure water on
my lips! . . . It is like pure water on my
hands. . . . Give me, give me thy hands! . . .
Oh, how small thy hands are! . . . I did not
know thou wert so beautiful! . . . I have never
seen anything so beautiful before thee. . . . I
was full of unrest; I sought throughout the
house. . . . I sought throughout the country.
. . . And I found not beauty. . . . And now I
have found thee! . . . I have found thee! . . .
I do not think there could be on the earth a
fairer woman! . . . Where art thou?—I no
longer hear thee breathe. . . .

MÉLISANDE.

Because I look on thee. . . .

PÉLLÉAS.

Why dost thou look so gravely on me?—We
are already in the shadow.—It is too dark
under this tree. Come into the light. We
cannot see how happy we are. Come, come;
so little time remains to us. . . .

MÉLISANDE.

No, no; let us stay here. . . . I am nearer thee in the dark. . . .

PÉLLÉAS.

Where are thine eyes? — Thou art not going to fly me? — Thou dost not think of me just now.

MÉLISANDE.

Oh, yes; oh, yes; I only think of thee. . . .

PÉLLÉAS.

Thou wert looking elsewhere. . . .

MÉLISANDE.

I saw thee elsewhere. . . .

PÉLLÉAS.

Thy soul is far away. . . . What ails thee, then? — Meseems thou art not happy. . . .

MÉLISANDE.

Yes, yes; I am happy, but I am sad. . . .

PÉLLÉAS.

One is sad often when one loves. . . .

MÉLISANDE.

I weep always when I think of thee. . . .

PÉLLÉAS.

I too. . . . I too, Mélisande. . . . I am
quite near thee; I weep for joy, and yet . . .
[*He kisses her again.*] — Thou art strange when
I kiss thee so. . . . Thou art so beautiful that
one would think thou wert about to die. . . .

MÉLISANDE.

Thou too. . . .

PÉLLÉAS.

There, there. . . . We do not what we
will. . . . I did not love thee the first time I saw
thee. . . .

MÉLISANDE.

Nor I. . . . nor I. . . . I was afraid. . . .

PÉLLÉAS.

I could not admit thine eyes. . . . I would
have gone away at once . . . and then . . .

MÉLISANDE.

And I, — I would not have come. . . . I do
not yet know why, — I was afraid to come. . . .

PÉLLÉAS.

There are so many things one never knows.
We are ever waiting; and then. . . . What is
that noise? — They are closing the gates! . . .

MÉLISANDE.

Yes, they have closed the gates. . . .

PÉLLÉAS.

We cannot go back now? — Hearest thou the
bolts? — Listen! listen! . . . the great chains!
. . . the great chains! . . . It is too late; it is
too late! . . .

MÉLISANDE.

All the better! all the better! all the
better! . . .

PÉLLÉAS.

Thou — . . . ? Behold, behold! . . . It is
no longer we who will it so! . . . All's lost,
all's saved! all is saved to-night! — Come,
come. . . . My heart beats like a madman, —
up to my very throat. . . . [*They embrace.*]
Listen! listen! my heart is almost strangling
me. . . . Come! come! . . . Ah, how beautiful
it is in the shadows! . . .

MÉLISANDE.

There is some one behind us! . . .

PÉLLEAS.

I see no one. . . .

MÉLISANDE.

I heard a noise. . . .

PÉLLÉAS.

I hear only thy heart in the dark. . . .

MÉLISANDE.

I heard the crackling of dead leaves. . . .

PELLÉAS.

Because the wind is silent all at once. . . .
It fell as we were kissing. . . .

MÉLISANDE.

How long our shadows are to-night ! . . .

PÉLLÉAS.

They embrace to the very end of the garden.
Oh, how they kiss far away from us ! . . .
Look ! look ! . . .

MÉLISANDE (*in a stifled voice*).

A-a-h ! — He is behind a tree !

PÉLLÉAS.

Who?

MÉLISANDE.

Golaud !

PÉLLÉAS.

Golaud ! — where? — I see nothing. . . .

MÉLISANDE.

There . . . at the end of our shadows. . . .

PÉLLÉAS.

Yes, yes; I saw him. . . . Let us not turn
abruptly. . . .

MÉLISANDE.

He has his sword. . . .

PÉLLÉAS.

I have not mine. . . .

MÉLISANDE.

He saw us kiss. . . .

PÉLLÉAS.

He does not know we have seen him. . . . Do not stir; do not turn your head. . . . He would rush headlong on us. . . . He will remain there while he thinks we do not know. He watches us. . . . He is still motionless. . . . Go, go at once this way. . . . I will wait for him. . . . I will stop him. . . .

MÉLISANDE.

No, no, no ! . . .

PÉLLÉAS.

Go ! go ! he has seen all ! . . . He will kill us ! . . .

MÉLISANDE.

All the better ! all the better ! all the better ! . . .

PÉLLÉAS.

He comes ! he comes ! . . . Thy mouth ! . . . Thy mouth ! . . .

MÉLISANDE.

Yes ! . . . yes ! yes ! . . .

[*They kiss desperatel*

PÉLLÉAS.

Oh ! oh !   All the stars are falling ! . . .

MÉLISANDE.

Upon me too ! upon me too ! . . .

PÉLLÉAS.

Again !   Again ! . . . Give ! give ! . . .

MÉLISANDE.

All ! all ! all ! . . .
[Golaud rushes upon them, sword in hand,
and strikes Pélléas, who falls at the brink of
the fountain.   Mélisande flees terrified.]

MÉLISANDE (*fleeing*).

Oh ! oh ! I have no courage ! . . . I have
no courage ! . . .
[GOLAUD *pursues her through the wood in
silence.*

ACT FIFTH.

Scene I. — *A lower hall in the castle. The women servants discovered, gathered together, while without children are playing before one of the ventilators of the hall.*

AN OLD SERVANT.

You will see, you will see, my daughters; it will be to-night. — Some one will come to tell us by and by. . . .

ANOTHER SERVANT.

They will not come to tell us . . . They don't know what they are doing any longer. . . .

THIRD SERVANT.

Let us wait here. . . .

FOURTH SERVANT.

We shall know well enough when we must go up. . . .

FIFTH SERVANT.

When the time is come, we shall go up of ourselves. . . .

SIXTH SERVANT.

There is no longer a sound heard in the house. . . .

SEVENTH SERVANT.

We ought to make the children keep still, who are playing before the ventilator.

EIGHTH SERVANT.

They will be still of themselves by and by.

NINTH SERVANT.

The time has not yet come. . . .

Enter an old Servant.

THE OLD SERVANT.

No one can go in the room any longer. I have listened more than an hour. . . . You could hear the flies walk on the doors. . . . I heard nothing. . . .

FIRST SERVANT.

Has she been left alone in the room?

THE OLD SERVANT.

No, no; I think the room is full of people.

FIRST SERVANT.

They will come, they will come, by and by. . . .

THE OLD SERVANT.

Lord! Lord! It is not happiness that has come into the house. . . . One may not speak, but if I could say what I know . . .

SECOND SERVANT.

It was you who found them before the gate?

THE OLD SERVANT.

Why, yes! why, yes! it was I who found them. The porter says it was he who saw them first; but it was I who waked them. He was sleeping on his face and would not get up. — And now he comes saying, "It was I who saw them first." Is that just? — See, I burned myself lighting a lamp to go down cellar. — Now what was I going to do down cellar? — I can't remember any more what I was going to do down cellar. — At any rate I got up very early; it was not yet very light; I said to myself, I will go across the courtyard, and then I will open the gate. Good; I go down the stairs on tiptoe, and I open the gate as if it were an ordinary gate. . . . My God! My God! What do I see? Divine a little what I see! . . .

FIRST SERVANT.

They were before the gate?

THE OLD SERVANT.

They were both stretched out before the gate! . . . Exactly like poor folk that are too

10

hungry. . . . They were huddled together like little children who are afraid. . . . The little princess was nearly dead, and the great Golaud had still his sword in his side. . . . There was blood on the sill. . . .

SECOND SERVANT.

We ought to make the children keep still. . . . They are screaming with all their might before the ventilator. . . .

THIRD SERVANT.

You can't hear yourself speak. . . .

FOURTH SERVANT.

There is nothing to be done : I have tried already ; they won't keep still. . . .

FIRST SERVANT.

It seems he is nearly cured?

THE OLD SERVANT.

Who?

FIRST SERVANT.

The great Golaud.

THIRD SERVANT.

Yes, yes ; they have taken him to his wife's room. I met them just now, in the corridor. They were holding him up as if he were drunk. He cannot yet walk alone.

THE OLD SERVANT.

He could not kill himself; he is too big.
But she is hardly wounded, and it is she who
is going to die. . . . Can you understand
that?

FIRST SERVANT.

You have seen the wound?

THE OLD SERVANT.

As I see you, my daughter. — I saw everything, you understand. . . . I saw it before all
the others. . . . A tiny little wound under her
little left breast, — a little wound that would n't
kill a pigeon.   Is it natural?

FIRST SERVANT.

Yes, yes; there is something underneath. . . .

SECOND SERVANT.

Yes; but she was delivered of her babe three
days ago. . . .

THE OLD SERVANT.

Exactly! . . . She was delivered on her
death-bed; is that a little sign? — And what a
child!   Have you seen it? — A wee little girl
a beggar would not bring into the world. . . .
A little wax figure that came much too soon; . . .
a little wax figure that must live in lambs' wool.
. . . Yes, yes; it is not happiness that has come
into the house. . . .

FIRST SERVANT.

Yes, yes ; it is the hand of God that has been stirring. . . .

SECOND SERVANT.

Yes, yes ; all that did not happen without reason. . . .

THIRD SERVANT.

It is as good lord Pélléas . . . where is he?
— No one knows. . . .

THE OLD SERVANT.

Yes, yes ; everybody knows. . . . But nobody dare speak of it. . . . One does not speak of this ; . . . one does not speak of that ; . . . one speaks no more of anything ; . . . one no longer speaks truth. . . . But *I* know he was found at the bottom of Blind Man's Spring ; . . . but no one, no one could see him. . . . Well, well, we shall only know all that at the last day. . . .

FIRST SERVANT.

I dare not sleep here any longer. . . .

THE OLD SERVANT.

Yes, yes ; once ill-fortune is in the house, one keeps silence in vain. . . .

THIRD SERVANT.

Yes ; it finds you all the same. . . .

THE OLD SERVANT.

Yes, yes; but we do not go where we would. . . .

FOURTH SERVANT.

Yes, yes; we do not do what we would. . . .

FIRST SERVANT.

They are afraid of us now. . . .

SECOND SERVANT.

They all keep silence. . . .

THIRD SERVANT.

They cast down their eyes in the corridors.

FOURTH SERVANT.

They do not speak any more except in a low voice.

FIFTH SERVANT.

You would think they had all done it together.

SIXTH SERVANT.

One does n't know what they have done. . . .

SEVENTH SERVANT.

What is to be done when the masters are afraid? . . .   [*A silence.*

FIRST SERVANT.

I no longer hear the children screaming.

SECOND SERVANT.

They are sitting down before the ventilator.

THIRD SERVANT.

They are huddled against each other.

THE OLD SERVANT.

I no longer hear anything in the house. . . .

FIRST SERVANT.

You no longer even hear the children breathe. . . .

THE OLD SERVANT.

Come, come ; it is time to go up. . . .

[*Exeunt, in silence.*

SCENE II. — *An apartment in the castle.* ARKËL, GOLAUD, *and the* PHYSICIAN *discovered in one corner of the room.* MÉLISANDE *is stretched upon her bed.*

THE PHYSICIAN.

It cannot be of that little wound she is dying ; a bird would not have died of it. . . . It is not you, then, who have killed her, good my lord ; do not be so disconsolate. . . . She could not have lived. . . . She was born without reason . . . to die ; and she dies without reason. . . . And then, it is not sure we shall not save her. . . .

ARKËL.

No, no; it seems to me we keep too silent, in spite of ourselves, in her room. . . . It is not a good sign. . . . Look how she sleeps . . . slowly, slowly; . . . it is as if her soul was cold forever. . . .

GOLAUD.

I have killed her without cause! I have killed her without cause! . . . Is it not enough to make the stones weep? . . . They had kissed like little children. . . . They had simply kissed. . . . They were brother and sister. . . . And I, and I at once! . . . I did it in spite of myself, look you. . . . I did it in spite of myself. . . .

THE PHYSICIAN.

Stop; I think she is waking. . . .

MÉLISANDE.

Open the window; . . . open the window. . . .

ARKËL

Shall I open this one, Mélisande?

MÉLISANDE.

No, no; the great window . . . the great window. . . . It is to see . . .

ARKËL.

Is not the sea air too cold to-night?

THE PHYSICIAN.

Do it; do it. . . .

MÉLISANDE.

Thanks. . . . Is it sunset?

ARKËL.

Yes; it is sunset on the sea; it is late.—
How are you, Mélisande?

MÉLISANDE.

Well, well. — Why do you ask that? I have
never been better. — And yet it seems to me I
know something. . . .

ARKËL.

What sayest thou? — I do not understand
thee. . . .

MÉLISANDE.

Neither do I understand all I say, you see.
. . . I do not know what I am saying. . . .
I do not know what I know. . . . I no longer
say what I would. . . .

ARKËL.

Why, yes! why, yes! . . . I am quite happy
to hear thee speak so; thou hast raved a little
these last days, and one no longer understood
thee. . . . But now all that is far away. . . .

MÉLISANDE.

I do not know. . . . — Are you all alone in the room, grandfather?

ARKËL.

No; there is the physician, besides, who cured thee. . . .

MÉLISANDE.

Ah ! . . .

ARKËL.

And then there is still some one else. . . .

MÉLISANDE.

Who is it?

ARKËL.

It is . . . thou must not be frightened. . . . He does not wish thee the least harm, be sure. . . . If thou 'rt afraid, he will go away. . . . He is very unhappy. . . .

MÉLISANDE.

Who is it?

ARKËL.

It is thy . . . thy husband. . . . It is Golaud. . . .

MÉLISANDE.

Golaud is here? Why does he not come by me?

GOLAUD (*dragging himself toward the bed*).

Mélisande . . . Mélisande. . . .

MÉLISANDE.

Is it you, Golaud? I should hardly recognize you any more. . . . It is the evening sunlight in my eyes. . . . Why look you on the walls? You have grown thin and old. . . . Is it a long while since we saw each other?

GOLAUD (*to* ARKËL *and the* PHYSICIAN).

Will you withdraw a moment, if you please, if you please? . . . I will leave the door wide open. . . . One moment only. . . . I would say something to her; else I could not die. . . . Will you? — Go clear to the end of the corridor; you can come back at once, at once. . . . Do not refuse me this. . . . I am a wretch. . . . [*Exit* ARKËL *and the* PHYSICIAN.] — Mélisande, hast thou pity on me, as I have pity on thee? . . . Mélisande? . . . Dost thou forgive me, Mélisande? . . .

MÉLISANDE.

Yes, yes, I do forgive thee. . . . What must I forgive? . . .

GOLAUD.

I have wrought thee so much ill, Mélisande. . . . I cannot tell thee the ill I have wrought thee. . . . But I see it, I see it so clearly to-day . . . since the first day. . . . And all I did not know till now leaps in my eyes to-night. . . . And it is all my fault, all that has happened, all that will happen. . . . If I could tell it, thou wouldst see as I do! . . . I see all! I

see all ! . . . But I loved thee so ! . . . I loved
thee so ! . . . But now there is some one dying.
. . . It is I who am dying. . . . And I would
know . . . I would ask thee. . . . Thou 'lt bear
me no ill-will . . . I would . . . The truth
must be told to a dying man. . . . He must
know the truth, or else he could not sleep. . . .
Swearest thou to tell me the truth?

MÉLISANDE.

Yes.

GOLAUD.

Didst thou love Pélléas?

MÉLISANDE.

Why, yes ; I loved him. — Where is he?

GOLAUD.

Thou dost not understand me? — Thou wilt
not understand me? — It seems to me . . . it
seems to me . . . Well, then, here : I ask thee
if thou lovedst him with a forbidden love? . . .
Wert thou . . . were you guilty?   Say, say, yes,
yes, yes ! . . .

MÉLISANDE.

No, no ; we were not guilty. — Why do you
ask that?

GOLAUD.

Mélisande ! . . . tell me the truth, for the
love of God !

MÉLISANDE.

Why have I not told the truth?

GOLAUD.

Do not lie so any more, at the moment of death !

MÉLISANDE.

Who is dying? — Is it I?

GOLAUD.

Thou, thou ! and I, I too, after thee ! . . . And we must have the truth. . . . We must have the truth at last, dost thou understand? . . . Tell me all ! Tell me all ! I forgive thee all ! . . .

MÉLISANDE.

Why am I going to die? — I did not know it. . . .

GOLAUD.

Thou knowest it now ! . . . It is time ! It is time ! . . . Quick ! quick ! . . . The truth ! the truth ! . . .

MÉLISANDE.

The truth . . . the truth . . .

GOLAUD.

Where art thou? — Mélisande ! — Where art thou? — It is not natural ! Mélisande ! Where art thou? — Where goest thou? [*Perceiving* ARKËL *and the* PHYSICIAN *at the door of the room.*] — Yes, yes; you may come in. . . . I know nothing; it is useless. . . . It is too late ; she is already too far away from us. . . . I shall never know ! . . . I shall die here like a blind man ! . . .

ARKËL.

What have you done? You will kill her. . . .

GOLAUD.

I have already killed her. . . .

ARKËL.

Mélisande. . . .

MÉLISANDE.

Is it you, grandfather?

ARKËL.

Yes, my daughter. . . . What would you have me do?

MÉLISANDE.

Is it true that the winter is beginning? . . .

ARKËL.

Why dost thou ask?

MÉLISANDE.

Because it is cold, and there are no more leaves. . . .

ARKËL.

Thou art cold?—Wilt thou have the windows closed?

MÉLISANDE.

No, no, . . . not till the sun be at the bottom of the sea.—It sinks slowly; then it is the winter beginning?

ARKËL.

Yes. — Thou dost not like the winter?

MÉLISANDE.

Oh! no.   I am afraid of the cold. — I am so afraid of the great cold. . . .

ARKËL.

Dost thou feel better?

MÉLISANDE.

Yes, yes; I have no longer all those qualms. . . .

ARKËL.

Wouldst thou see thy child?

MÉLISANDE.

What child?

ARKËL.

Thy child. — Thou art a mother. . . . Thou hast brought a little daughter into the world. . . .

MÉLISANDE.

Where is she?

ARKËL.

Here. . . .

MÉLISANDE.

It is strange. . . . I cannot lift my arms to take her. . . .

ARKËL.

Because you are still very weak. . . . I will
hold her myself; look. . . .

MÉLISANDE.

She does not laugh. . . . She is little. . . .
She is going to weep too. . . . I pity her. . . .
[The room has been invaded, little by little, by
the women servants of the castle, who range
themselves in silence along the walls and
wait.]

GOLAUD (*rising abruptly*).

What is the matter?—What are all these
women coming here for? . . .

THE PHYSICIAN.

It is the servants. . . .

ARKËL.

Who was it called them?

THE PHYSICIAN.

It was not I. . . .

GOLAUD.

Why do you come here?—No one has asked
for you. . . . What come you here to do?—
But what is it, then?—Answer me! . . .
[*The servants make no answer.*

ARKËL.

Do not speak too loud. . . . She is going to
sleep; she has closed her eyes. . . .

GOLAUD.

It is not . . . ?

THE PHYSICIAN.

No, no; see, she breathes. . . .

ARKËL.

Her eyes are full of tears. — It is her soul weeping now. . . . Why does she stretch her arms out so? — What would she?

THE PHYSICIAN.

It is toward the child, without doubt. . . . It is the struggle of motherhood against . . .

GOLAUD.

At this moment? — At this moment? — You must say. Say! Say! . . .

THE PHYSICIAN.

Perhaps.

GOLAUD.

At once? . . . Oh! oh! I must tell her. . . . — Mélisande! Mélisande! . . . Leave me alone! leave me alone with her! . . .

ARKËL.

No, no; do not come near. . . . Trouble her not. . . . Speak no more to her. . . . You know not what the soul is. . . .

GOLAUD.

It is not my fault! . . . It is not my fault!

ARKËL.

Hush! . . . Hush! . . . We must speak softly now. — She must not be disturbed. . . . The human soul is very silent. . . . The human soul likes to depart alone. . . . It suffers so timorously. . . . But the sadness, Golaud . . . the sadness of all we see! . . . Oh! oh! oh! . . .

> [*At this moment, all the servants fall suddenly on their knees at the back of the chamber.*]

ARKËL (*turning*).

What is the matter?

THE PHYSICIAN (*approaching the bed and feeling the body*).

They are right. . . .

> [*A long silence.*

ARKËL.

I saw nothing. — Are you sure? . . .

THE PHYSICIAN.

Yes, yes.

ARKËL.

I heard nothing. . . . So quick, so quick! . . . All at once! . . . She goes without a word. . . .

GOLAUD (*sobbing*).

Oh! oh! oh!

11

ARKËL.

Do not stay here, Golaud. . . . She must
have silence now. . . . Come, come. . . . It
is terrible, but it is not your fault. . . . 'T was
a little being, so quiet, so fearful, and so silent.
. . . 'T was a poor little mysterious being, like
everybody. . . . She lies there as if she were
the big sister of her child. . . . Come, come.
. . . My God! My God! . . . I shall never
understand it at all. . . . Let us not stay here.
— Come; the child must not stay here in this
room. . . . She must live now in her place.
. . . It is the poor little one's turn. . . .

[*They go out in silence.*

[CURTAIN.]

Home.

To Mademoiselle Sara de Swart.

Persons.

IN THE GARDEN.

THE OLD MAN.
THE STRANGER.
MARTHA
AND MARY, } *granddaughters of the old man.*
A PEASANT.
THE CROWD.

IN THE HOUSE.

THE FATHER,
THE MOTHER,
THE TWO DAUGHTERS, } *Silent characters.*
THE CHILD,

Home.

—◆—

[An old garden, planted with willows. At the
back, a house in which three windows on the
ground-floor are lighted. A family, sitting
up under the lamp, is seen rather distinctly.
The father is seated by the fireside. The
mother, one elbow on the table, is staring
into space. Two young girls, clad in white,
embroider, dream, and smile in the quiet of
the room. A child lies asleep with his head
under the mother's left arm. Whenever one
of them rises, walks, or makes a gesture, his
movements seem to be grave, slow, rare,
and, as it were, spiritualized by the distance,
the light, and the vague veil of the windows.
  The old man and the stranger enter the
garden cautiously.]

THE OLD MAN.

We are in the part of the garden behind the
house. They never come here. The doors are
on the other side. — They are closed, and the
shutters are up. But there are no shutters on
this side, and I saw a light. . . . Yes ; they
are sitting up still under the lamp. It is fortunate they have not heard us ; the mother or the
young girls would have come out, perhaps, and
then what should we have done ? . . .

THE STRANGER.

What are we going to do?

THE OLD MAN.

I should like to see, first, if they are all in the room. Yes, I see the father sitting in the chimney-corner. He waits, with his hands on his knees; . . . the mother is resting her elbow on the table.

THE STRANGER.

She is looking at us. . . .

THE OLD MAN.

No; she doesn't know where she is looking: her eyes do not wink. She cannot see us; we are in the shade of great trees. But do not go any nearer. . . . The two sisters of the dead girl are in the room too. They are embroidering slowly; and the little child is asleep. It is nine by the clock in the corner. . . . They suspect nothing, and they do not speak.

THE STRANGER.

If one could draw the father's attention, and make him some sign? He has turned his head this way. Would you like me to knock at one of the windows? One of them ought to be told before the others. . . .

THE OLD MAN.

I don't know which one to choose. . . . We must take great precautions. . . . The father is

old and ailing. . . . So is the mother; and the
sisters are too young. . . . And they all loved
her with such love as will never be again. . . .
I never saw a happier household. . . . No, no,
do not go near the window; that would be
worse than anything else. . . . It is better to
announce it as simply as possible, — as if it were
an ordinary event, — and not to look too sad;
for otherwise their grief will wish to be greater
than yours and will know of nothing more that
it can do. . . . Let us go on the other side of
the garden. We will knock at the door and go
in as if nothing had happened. I will go in
first: they will not be surprised to see me; I
come sometimes in the evening, to bring them
flowers or fruit, and pass a few hours with them.

THE STRANGER.

Why must I go with you? Go alone; I will
wait till I am called. . . . They have never
seen me. . . . I am only a passer-by; I am a
stranger. . . .

THE OLD MAN.

It is better not to be alone. A sorrow that
one does not bring alone is not so unmixed nor
so heavy. . . . I was thinking of that as we
were coming here. . . . If I go in alone, I
shall have to be speaking from the first minute;
in a few words they will know everything, and I
shall have nothing more to say; and I am
afraid of the silence following the last words
that announce a woe. . . . It is then the heart

is rent. . . . If we go in together, I shall
tell them, for example, after going a long
way about, "She was found so. . . . She was
floating in the river, and her hands were
clasped." . . .

THE STRANGER.

Her hands were not clasped; her arms were
hanging down along her body.

THE OLD MAN.

You see, one speaks in spite of oneself. . . .
And the sorrow is lost in the details; . . . but
otherwise, if I go in alone, at the first words,
knowing them as I do, it would be dreadful, and
God knows what might happen. . . . But if we
speak in turn, they will listen to us and not
think to look the ill news in the face. . . . Do
not forget the mother will be there, and that her
life hangs by a thread. . . . It is good that the
first wave break on some unnecessary words.
. . . There should be a little talking around
the unhappy, and they should have people
about them. . . . The most indifferent bear unwittingly a part of the grief. . . . So, without
noise or effort, it divides, like air or light. . . .

THE STRANGER.

Your clothes are wet through; they are
dripping on the flagstones.

THE OLD MAN.

It is only the bottom of my cloak that dipped
in the water. — You seem to be cold. Your

chest is covered with earth. . . . I did not notice it on the road on account of the darkness. . . .

THE STRANGER.

I went into the water up to my waist.

THE OLD MAN.

Was it long after you found her when I came?

THE STRANGER.

A few minutes, barely. I was going toward the village; it was already late, and the bank was getting dark. I was walking with my eyes fixed on the river because it was lighter than the road, when I saw something strange a step or two from a clump of reeds. . . . I drew near and made out her hair, which had risen almost in a circle above her head, and whirled round, so, in the current.

[*In the room, the two young girls turn their heads toward the window.*]

THE OLD MAN.

Did you see the two sisters' hair quiver on their shoulders?

THE STRANGER.

They turned their heads this way. . . . They simply turned their heads. Perhaps I spoke too loud. [*The two young girls resume their former position.*] But they are already looking no longer. . . . I went into the water up to my

waist and I was able to take her by the hand
and pull her without effort to the shore. . . .
She was as beautiful as her sisters are.

THE OLD MAN.

She was perhaps more beautiful. . . . I do
not know why I have lost all courage. . . .

THE STRANGER.

What courage are you talking of? We have
done all man could do. . . . She was dead
more than an hour ago. . . .

THE OLD MAN.

She was alive this morning! . . . I met her
coming out of church. . . . She told me she
was going away; she was going to see her
grandmother on the other side of the river
where you found her. . . . She did not know
when I should see her again. . . . She must
have been on the point of asking me something;
then she dared not and left me abruptly. But
I think of it now. . . . And I saw nothing!
. . . She smiled as they smile who choose to
be silent, or who are afraid they will not be
understood. . . . She seemed hardly to hope.
. . . Her eyes were not clear and hardly looked
at me. . . .

THE STRANGER.

Some peasants told me they had seen her
wandering on the river-bank until nightfall. . . .
They thought she was looking for flowers. . . .
It may be that her death . . .

THE OLD MAN.

We cannot tell. . . . What is there we can
tell? . . . She was perhaps of those who do
not wish to speak, and every one of us bears in
himself more than one reason for no longer
living. . . . We cannot see in the soul as we
see in that room. They are all like that. . . .
They only say trite things; and no one suspects
aught. . . . You live for months by some one
who is no longer of this world and whose soul
can bend no longer; you answer without thinking; and you see what happens. . . . They
look like motionless dolls, and, oh, the events
that take place in their souls! . . . They do
not know themselves what they are. . . . She
would have lived as the rest live. . . . She
would have said up to her death: " Monsieur,
Madame, we shall have rain this morning," or
else, " We are going to breakfast; we shall be
thirteen at table," or else : " The fruits are not
yet ripe." They speak with a smile of the
flowers that have fallen, and weep in the dark.
. . . An angel even would not see what should
be seen; and man only understands when it is
too late. . . . Yesterday evening she was there,
under the lamp like her sisters, and you would
not see them as they should be seen, if this had
not occurred. . . . I seem to see her now for
the first time. . . . Something must be added to
common life before we can understand it. . . .
They are beside you day and night, and you
perceive them only at the moment when they

depart forever. . . . And yet the strange little soul she must have had; the poor, naïve, exhaustless little soul she had, my son, if she said what she must have said, if she did what she must have done ! . . .

THE STRANGER.

Just now they are smiling in silence in the room. . . .

THE OLD MAN.

They are at peace. . . . They did not expect her to-night. . . .

THE STRANGER.

They smile without stirring ; . . . and see, the father is putting his finger on his lips. . . .

THE OLD MAN.

He is calling attention to the child asleep on its mother's heart. . . .

THE STRANGER.

She dares not raise her eyes lest she disturb its sleep. . . .

THE OLD MAN.

They are no longer working. . . . A great silence reigns. . . .

THE STRANGER.

They have let fall the skein of white silk. . . .

THE OLD MAN.

They are watching the child. . . .

THE STRANGER.

They do not know that others are watching them. . . .

THE OLD MAN.

We are watched too. . . .

THE STRANGER.

They have lifted their eyes. . . .

THE OLD MAN.

And yet they can see nothing. . . .

THE STRANGER.

They seem happy; and yet nobody knows what may be — . . .

THE OLD MAN.

They think themselves in safety. . . . They have shut the doors; and the windows have iron bars. . . . They have mended the walls of the old house; they have put bolts upon the oaken doors. . . . They have foreseen all that could be foreseen. . . .

THE STRANGER.

We must end by telling them. . . . Some one might come and let them know abruptly. . . . There was a crowd of peasants in the

meadow where the dead girl was found. . . .
If one of them knocked at the door . . .

THE OLD MAN.

Martha and Mary are beside the poor dead
child. The peasants were to make a litter of
leaves; and I told the elder to come warn us
in all haste, the moment they began their
march. Let us wait till she comes; she will go
in with me. . . . We should not have looked
on them so. . . . I thought it would be only to
knock upon the door; to go in simply, find a
phrase or two, and tell. . . . But I have seen
them live too long under their lamp. . . .

Enter MARY.

MARY.

They are coming, grandfather.

THE OLD MAN.

Is it you? — Where are they?

MARY.

They are at the foot of the last hills.

THE OLD MAN.

They will come in silence?

MARY.

I told them to pray in a low voice. Martha
is with them. . . .

THE OLD MAN.

Are they many?

MARY.

The whole village is about the bearers. They had brought lights. I told them to put them out. . . .

THE OLD MAN.

Which way are they coming?

MARY.

They are coming by the footpaths. They are walking slowly. . . .

THE OLD MAN.

It is time. . . .

MARY.

You have told them, grandfather?

THE OLD MAN.

You see plainly we have told them nothing. . . . They are waiting still under the lamp. . . . Look, my child, look! You will see something of life. . . .

MARY.

Oh, how at peace they seem! . . . You would say I saw them in a dream. . . .

THE STRANGER.

Take care, I saw both sisters give a start. . . .

THE OLD MAN.

They are getting up. . . .

THE STRANGER.

I think they are coming to the windows. . . .
> [At this moment, one of the two sisters of whom
> they speak draws near the first window, the
> other near the third, and, pressing their
> hands at the same time against the panes,
> look a long while into the darkness.]

THE OLD MAN.

No one comes to the window in the middle. . . .

MARY.

They are looking. . . . They are listening. . . .

THE OLD MAN.

The elder smiles at what she does not see.

THE STRANGER.

And the other has eyes full of fearfulness. . . .

THE OLD MAN.

Take care ; we do not know how far the soul extends about men. . . .
> [*A long silence.* MARY *cowers against
> the old man's breast and kisses him.*]

MARY.

Grandfather ! . . .

THE OLD MAN.

Do not weep, my child. . . . We shall have our turn. . . .

[*A silence.*

THE STRANGER.

They are looking a long while. . . .

THE OLD MAN.

They might look a hundred thousand years and not perceive anything, the poor little sisters. . . . The night is too dark. . . . They are looking this way; and it is from that way the misfortune is coming. . . .

THE STRANGER.

It is fortunate they look this way. . . . I do not know what that is coming toward us, over by the meadows.

MARY.

I think it is the crowd. . . . They are so far away you can hardly make them out. . . .

THE STRANGER.

They follow the undulations of the path. . . . Now they appear again on a hillside in the moonlight. . .

MARY.

Oh, how many they seem! . . . They had already run up from the suburbs of the city when I came. . . . They are going a long way around. . . .

THE OLD MAN.

They will come in spite of all: I see them too. . . . They are on the march across the meadow lands. . . . They seem so small you hardly make them out among the grasses. . . . They look like children playing in the moonlight; and if the girls should see them, they would not understand. . . . In vain they turn their backs; those yonder draw near with every step they take, and the sorrow has been growing these two hours already. They cannot hinder it from growing; and they that bear it there no longer can arrest it. . . . It is their master too, and they must serve it. . . . It has its end and follows its own road. . . . It is unwearying and has but one idea. . . . Needs must they lend their strength. They are sad, but they come. . . . They have pity, but they must go forward. . . .

MARY.

The elder smiles no longer, grandfather. . . .

THE STRANGER.

They leave the windows. . . .

MARY.

They kiss their mother. . . .

THE STRANGER.

The elder has caressed the curls of the child without waking him. . . .

MARY.

Oh! the father wants to be kissed too. . . .

THE STRANGER.

And now silence. . . .

MARY.

They come back beside the mother. . . .

THE STRANGER.

And the father follows the great pendulum of the clock with his eyes. . . .

MARY.

You would say they were praying without knowing what they did. . . .

THE STRANGER.

You would say that they were listening to their souls. . . .

[*A silence.*

MARY.

Grandfather, don't tell them to-night! . . .

THE OLD MAN.

You see, you too lose courage. . . . I knew well that we must not look.   I am nearly eighty-three years old, and this is the first time the sight of life has struck me.   I do not know why everything they do seems so strange and grave to me. . . . They wait for night quite simply, under their lamp, as we might have been waiting under ours;

and yet I seem to see them from the height of
another world, because I know a little truth
which they do not know yet. . . . Is it that, my
children? Tell me, then, why you are pale,
too? Is there something else, perhaps, that
cannot be told and causes us to weep? I did
not know there was anything so sad in life, nor
that it frightened those who looked upon it. . . .
And nothing can have occurred that I should be
afraid to see them so at peace. . . . They have
too much confidence in this world. . . . There
they are, separated from the enemy by a poor
window. . . . They think nothing will happen
because they have shut the door, and do not
know that something is always happening in our
souls, and that the world does not end at the
doors of our houses. . . . They are so sure of
their little life and do not suspect how many
others know more of it than they; and that I,
poor old man, — I hold here, two steps from their
door, all their little happiness, like a sick bird,
in my old hands I do not dare to open. . . .

MARY.

Have pity, grandfather. . . .

THE OLD MAN.

We have pity on them, my child, but no one
has pity on us. . . .

MARY.

Tell them to-morrow, grandfather; tell them
when it is light. . . . They will not be so sorrow-
ful. . . .

THE OLD MAN.

Perhaps you are right, my child. . . . It would be better to leave all this in the night. And the light is sweet to sorrow. . . . But what would they say to us to-morrow? Misfortune renders jealous; they whom it strikes, wish to be told before strangers; they do not like to have it left in the hands of those they do not know. . . . We should look as if we had stolen something. . . .

THE STRANGER.

There is no more time, besides; I hear the murmur of prayers already. . . .

MARY.

There they are. . . . They are passing behind the hedges. . . .

Enter MARTHA.

MARTHA.

Here I am. I have brought them this far. I have told them to wait on the road. [*Cries of children heard*.] Ah! the children are crying again. . . . I forbade their coming. . . . But they wanted to see too, and the mothers would not obey. . . . I will go tell them. . . . No; they are silent. — Is everything ready? — I have brought the little ring that was found on her. . . . I have some fruit, too, for the child. . . . I laid her out myself on the litter. She looks as if she were asleep. . . . I had a good deal of trouble; her hair would not obey. . . . I had some marguerites plucked. . . . It is sad, there were no other flowers. . . . What are you doing here? Why are you not by them? . . . [*She looks at the windows.*] They do not weep? . . . They . . . you have not told them?

THE OLD MAN.

Martha, Martha, there is too much life in your soul; you cannot understand. . . .

MARTHA.

Why should I not understand? . . . [*After a silence and in a tone of very grave reproach.*] You cannot have done that, grandfather. . . .

THE OLD MAN.

Martha, you do not know. . . .

MARTHA.

I will tell them.

THE OLD MAN.

Stay here, my child, and look at them a moment.

MARTHA.

Oh, how unhappy they are! . . . They can wait no longer.

THE OLD MAN.

Why?

MARTHA.

I do not know; . . . it is no longer possible! . . .

THE OLD MAN.

Come here, my child. . . .

MARTHA.

How patient they are !

THE OLD MAN.

Come here, my child. . . .

MARTHA.

[*Turning.*]   Where are you, grandfather?   I
am so unhappy I cannot see you any more.
. . . I do not know what to do myself any
more. . . .

THE OLD MAN.

Do not look at them any more; till they
know all. . . .

MARTHA.

I will go in with you. . . .

THE OLD MAN.

No, Martha, stay here. . . . Sit beside your
sister, on this old stone bench, against the wall
of the house, and do not look. . . . You are
too young; you never could forget. . . . You
cannot know what a face is like at the moment
when death passes before its eyes. . . . There
will be cries, perhaps. . . . Do not turn round.
. . . Perhaps there will be nothing. . . . Above
all, do not turn if you hear nothing. . . . One
does not know the course of grief beforehand.
. . . A few little deep-rooted sobs, and that is all,

usually. . . . I do not know myself what I may do when I shall hear them. . . . That belongs no longer to this life. . . . Kiss me, my child, before I go away. . . .

> [The murmur of prayers has gradually drawn nearer. Part of the crowd invades the garden. Dull steps heard, running, and low voices speaking.]

THE STRANGER (*to the crowd*).

Stay here ; . . . do not go near the windows. . . . Where is she? . . .

A PEASANT.

Who?

THE STRANGER.

The rest . . . the bearers? . . .

THE PEASANT.

They are coming by the walk that leads to the door.

> [The old man goes away. Martha and Mary are seated on the bench, with their backs turned to the windows. Murmurs in the crowd.]

THE STRANGER.

S—t! . . . Do not speak.

> [*The elder of the two sisters rises and goes to bolt the door. . . .*]

MARTHA.

She opens it?

THE STRANGER.

On the contrary, she is shutting it.

[*A silence.*

MARTHA.

Grandfather has not entered?

THE STRANGER.

No. . . . She returns and sits down by her mother. . . . The others do not stir, and the child sleeps all the time. . . .

[*A silence.*

MARTHA.

Sister, give me your hands. . . .

MARY.

Martha! . . .

[*They embrace and give each other a kiss.*

THE STRANGER.

He must have knocked. . . . They have all raised their heads at the same time; . . . they look at each other. . . .

MARTHA.

Oh! oh! my poor little sister! . . . I shall cry too! . . .

[*She stifles her sobs on her sister's shoulder.*

THE STRANGER.

He must be knocking again. . . . The father looks at the clock. He rises.

MARTHA.

Sister, sister, I want to go in too. . . . They cannot be alone any longer. . . .

MARY.

Martha! Martha! . . .

[*She holds her back.*

THE STRANGER.

The father is at the door. . . . He draws the bolts. . . . He opens the door prudently. . . .

MARTHA.

Oh! . . . you do not see the . . .

THE STRANGER.

What?

MARTHA.

Those who bear. . . .

THE STRANGER.

He hardly opens it. . . . I can only see a corner of the lawn; and the fountain. . . . He does not let go the door; . . . he steps back. . . . He looks as if he were saying: "Ah, it's you!" . . . He raises his arms. . . . He shuts the door again carefully. . . . Your grandfather has come into the room. . . .

[The crowd has drawn nearer the windows. Martha and Mary half rise at first, then draw near also, clasping each other tightly. The old man is seen advancing into the room. The two sisters of the dead girl rise; the

mother rises as well, after laying the child
carefully in the armchair she has just abandoned; in such a way that from without
the little one may be seen asleep, with his
head hanging a little to one side, in the
centre of the room. The mother advances
to meet the old man and extends her hand to
him, but draws it back before he has had
time to take it. One of the young girls
offers to take off the visitor's cloak and the
other brings forward a chair for him; but
the old man makes a slight gesture of re-
fusal. The father smiles with a surprised
look. The old man looks toward the
windows.

THE STRANGER.

He dares not tell them. . . . He has looked
at us. . . .

[*Rumors in the crowd.*

THE STRANGER.

S . . . t ! . . .
[The old man, seeing their faces at the windows, has quickly turned his eyes away. As
one of the young girls continues to offer him
the same armchair, he ends by sitting down
and passes his right hand across his forehead
several times.]

THE STRANGER.

He sits down. . . .
[The other people in the room sit down also,
while the father talks volubly. At last the
old man opens his mouth, and the tone of his
voice seems to attract attention. But the
father interrupts him. The old man begins
to speak again, and little by little the others
become motionless. All at once, the mother
starts and rises.]

MARTHA.

Oh ! the mother is going to understand ! . . .
> [She turns away and hides her face in her
> hands. New murmurs in the crowd. They
> elbow each other. Children cry to be lifted
> up, so that they may see too. Most of the
> mothers obey.]

THE STRANGER.

S . . . t ! . . . He has not told them yet. . . .
> [The mother is seen to question the old man
> in anguish. He says a few words more;
> then abruptly all the rest rise too and seem
> to question him. He makes a slow sign of
> affirmation with his head.]

THE STRANGER.

He has told them. . . . He has told them
all at once ! . . .

VOICES IN THE CROWD.

He has told them ! . . . He has told
them ! . . .

THE STRANGER.

You hear nothing. . . .
> [The old man rises too, and, without turning,
> points with his finger to the door behind him.
> The mother, the father, and the two young
> girls throw themselves on this door, which
> the father cannot at once succeed in open-
> ing. The old man tries to prevent the
> mother from going out.

VOICES IN THE CROWD.

They are going out ! They are going
out ! . . .
> [Jostling in the garden. All rush to the other
> side of the house and disappear, with the

exception of the stranger, who remains at
the windows. In the room, both sides of the
folding-door at last open ; all go out at the
same time. Beyond can be seen a starry
sky, the lawn and the fountain in the moonlight, while in the middle of the abandoned
room the child continues to sleep peacefully
in the armchair. — Silence.]

THE STRANGER.

The child has not waked ! . . .

[*He goes out also.*

[CURTAIN.]

The Death of Tintagiles.

To A. F. Lugné-Poe.

Persons.

Tintagiles.

Ygraine,
Bellangère, } *sisters of Tintagiles.*

Aglovale.

Three Servants of the Queen.

The Death of Tintagiles.

—◆—

ACT FIRST.

At the top of a hill, overlooking the castle.

Enter YGRAINE, *holding* TINTAGILES *by the hand.*

YGRAINE.

Thy first night will be troubled, Tintagiles.
Already the sea howls about us; and the trees
are moaning. It is late. The moon is just
setting behind the poplars that stifle the palace.
. . . We are alone, perhaps, for all that here
we have to live on guard. There seems to be
a watch set for the approach of the slightest
happiness. I said to myself one day, in the
very depths of my soul, — and God himself could
hardly hear it, — I said to myself one day I
should be happy. . . . There needed nothing
further; in a little while our old father died,
and both our brothers vanished without a single
human being able since to tell us where they
are. Now I am all alone, with my poor sister
and thee, my little Tintagiles; and I have no

faith in the future. . . . Come here; sit on my knee. Kiss me first; and put thy little arms, there, all the way around my neck; . . . perhaps they will not be able to undo them. . . . Rememberest thou the time when it was I that carried thee at night when bedtime came; and when thou fearedst the shadows of my lamp in the long windowless corridors?— I felt my soul tremble upon my lips when I saw thee, suddenly, this morning. . . . I thought thee so far away, and so secure. . . . Who was it made thee come here?

TINTAGILES.

I do not know, little sister.

YGRAINE.

Thou dost not know any longer what was said?

TINTAGILES.

They said I had to leave.

YGRAINE.

But why hadst thou to leave?

TINTAGILES.

Because it was the Queen's will.

YGRAINE.

They did not say why it was her will?— I am sure they said many things. . . .

TINTAGILES.

I heard nothing, little sister.

YGRAINE.

When they spoke among themselves, what did they say?

TINTAGILES.

They spoke in a low voice, little sister.

YGRAINE.

All the time?

TINTAGILES.

All the time, sister Ygraine; except when they looked at me.

YGRAINE.

They did not speak of the Queen?

TINTAGILES.

They said she was never seen, sister Ygraine.

YGRAINE.

And those who were with thee, on the bridge of the ship, said nothing?

TINTAGILES.

They minded nothing but the wind and the sails, sister Ygraine.

YGRAINE.

Ah! . . . That does not astonish me, my child. . . .

TINTAGILES.

They left me all alone, little sister.

YGRAINE.

Listen, Tintagiles, I will tell thee what I know. . . .

TINTAGILES.

What dost thou know, sister Ygraine?

YGRAINE.

Not much, my child. . . . My sister and I have crept along here, since our birth, without daring to understand a whit of all that happens. . . . For a long while indeed, I lived like a blind woman on this island; and it all seemed natural to me. . . . I saw no other events than the flying of a bird, the trembling of a leaf, the opening of a rose. . . . There reigned such a silence that the falling of a ripe fruit in the park called faces to the windows. . . . And no one seemed to have the least suspicion; . . . but one night I learned there must be something else. . . . I would have fled, and could not. . . . Hast thou understood what I have said?

TINTAGILES.

Yes, yes, little sister; I understand whatever you will. . . .

YGRAINE.

Well, then, let us speak no more of things that are not known. . . . Thou seest yonder,

behind the dead trees that poison the horizon,
— thou seest the castle yonder, in the depth
of the valley?

TINTAGILES.

That which is so black, sister Ygraine?

YGRAINE.

It is black indeed. . . . It is at the very
depth of an amphitheatre of shadows. . . . We
have to live there. . . . It might have been
built on the summit of the great mountains that
surround it. . . . The mountains are blue all
day. . . . We should have breathed. We
should have seen the sea and the meadows on
the other side of the rocks. . . . But they preferred to put it in the depth of the valley; and
the very air does not go down so low. . . . It
is falling in ruins, and nobody bewares. . . .
The walls are cracking; you would say it was
dissolving in the shadows. . . . There is only
one tower unassailed by the weather. . . . It is
enormous; and the house never comes out of
its shadow. . . .

TINTAGILES.

There is something shining, sister Ygraine.
. . . See, see, the great red windows! . . .

YGRAINE.

They are those of the tower, Tintagiles: they
are the only ones where you will see light; it
is there the throne of the Queen is set.

TINTAGILES.

I shall not see the Queen?

YGRAINE.

No one can see her. . . .

TINTAGILES.

Why can't one see her?

YGRAINE.

Come nearer, Tintagiles. . . . Not a bird nor a blade of grass must hear us. . . .

TINTAGILES.

There is no grass, little sister. . . . [*A silence.*] —What does the Queen do?

YGRAINE.

No one knows, my child. She does not show herself. . . . She lives there, all alone in her tower; and they that serve her do not go out by day. . . . She is very old; she is the mother of our mother; and she would reign alone. . . . She is jealous and suspicious, and they say that she is mad. . . . She fears lest some one rise into her place; and it was doubtless because of that fear that she had thee brought hither. . . . Her orders are carried out no one knows how. . . . She never comes down; and all the doors of the tower are closed night and day. . . . I never caught a glimpse of her; but others have seen her, it seems, in the past, when she was young. . . .

TINTAGILES.

Is she very ugly, sister Ygraine?

YGRAINE.

They say she is not beautiful, and that she is growing huge. . . . But they that have seen her dare never speak of it. . . . Who knows, indeed, if they have seen her? . . . She has a power not to be understood; and we live here with a great unpitying weight upon our souls. . . . Thou must not be frightened beyond measure, nor have bad dreams; we shall watch over thee, my little Tintagiles, and no evil will be able to reach thee; but do not go far from me, your sister Bellangère, nor our old master Aglovale. . . .

TINTAGILES.

Not from Aglovale either, sister Ygraine?

YGRAINE.

Not from Aglovale either. . . . He loves us. . . .

TINTAGILES.

He is so old, little sister!

YGRAINE.

He is old, but very wise. . . . He is the only friend we have left; and he knows many things. . . . It is strange; she has made thee come hither without letting any one know. . . . I do not know what there is in my heart. . . . I was sorry and glad to know thou wert so far away, beyond the sea. . . . And now . . . I was astonished. . . . I went out this morning to see if the sun was rising over the mountains; and it is thou I see upon the threshold. . . . I knew thee at once. . . .

TINTAGILES.

No, no, little sister; it was I that laughed first. . . .

YGRAINE.

I could not laugh at once. . . . Thou wilt understand. . . . It is time, Tintagiles, and the wind is growing black upon the sea. . . . Kiss me harder, again, again, before thou stand'st upright. . . . Thou knowest not how we love. . . . Give me thy little hand. . . . I shall guard it well; and we will go back into the sickening castle.

[*Exeunt.*

ACT SECOND.

An apartment in the castle. AGLOVALE *and* YGRAINE *discovered.*

Enter BELLANGÈRE.

BELLANGÈRE.

Where is Tintagiles?

YGRAINE.

Here; do not speak too loud. He sleeps in the other room. He seems a little pale, a little ailing too. He was tired by the journey and the long sea-voyage. Or else the atmosphere of the castle has startled his little soul. He cried for no cause. I rocked him to sleep on my knees; come, see. . . . He sleeps in our bed. . . . He sleeps very gravely, with one hand on his forehead, like a little sad king. . . .

BELLANGÈRE (*bursting suddenly into tears*).

My sister! my sister! . . . my poor sister! . . .

YGRAINE.

What is the matter?

BELLANGÈRE.

I dare not say what I know, . . . and I am
not sure that I know anything, . . . and yet I
heard that which one could not hear. . . .

YGRAINE.

What didst thou hear?

BELLANGÈRE.

I was passing near the corridors of the
tower. . . .

YGRAINE.

Ah! . . .

BELLANGÈRE.

A door there was ajar. I pushed it very
softly. . . . I went in. . . .

YGRAINE.

In where?

BELLANGÈRE.

I had never seen the place. . . . There were
other corridors lighted with lamps; then low
galleries that had no outlet. . . . I knew it was
forbidden to go on. . . . I was afraid, and I
was going to return upon my steps, when I
heard a sound of voices one could hardly
hear. . . .

YGRAINE.

It must have been the handmaids of the
Queen; they dwell at the foot of the tower. . . .

BELLANGÈRE.

I do not know just what it was. . . . There must have been more than one door between us; and the voices came to me like the voice of some one who was being smothered. . . . I drew as near as I could. . . . I am not sure of anything, but I think they spoke of a child that came to-day and of a crown of gold. . . . They seemed to be laughing. . . .

YGRAINE.

They laughed?

BELLANGÈRE.

Yes, I think they laughed . . . unless they were weeping, or unless it was something I did not understand; for it was hard to hear, and their voices were sweet. . . . They seemed to echo in a crowd under the arches. . . . They spoke of the child the Queen would see. . . . They will probably come up this evening. . . .

YGRAINE.

What? . . . This evening? . . .

BELLANGÈRE.

Yes. . . . Yes. . . . I think so. . . .

YGRAINE.

They spoke no one's name?

BELLANGÈRE.

They spoke of a child, of a very little child. . . .

YGRAINE.

There is no other child. . . .

BELLANGÈRE.

They raised their voices a little at that moment, because one of them had said the day seemed not yet come. . . .

YGRAINE.

I know what that means; it is not the first time they have issued from the tower. . . . I knew well why she made him come; . . . but I could not believe she would hasten so! . . . We shall see; . . . we are three, and we have time. . . .

BELLANGÈRE.

What wilt thou do?

YGRAINE.

I do not know yet what I shall do, but I will astonish her. . . . Do you know how you tremble? . . . I will tell you. . . .

BELLANGÈRE.

What?

YGRAINE.

She shall not take him without trouble. . . .

BELLANGÈRE.

We are alone, sister Ygraine. . . .

YGRAINE.

Ah! it is true, we are alone! . . . There is
but one remedy, the one with which we have
always succeeded! . . . Let us wait upon our
knees as the other times. . . . Perhaps she will
have pity! . . . She allows herself to be dis-
armed by tears. . . . We must grant her all she
asks us; haply she will smile; and she is wont
to spare all those who kneel. . . . She has been
there for years in her huge tower, devouring our
beloved, and none, not one, has dared to strike
her in the face. . . . She is there, upon our
souls, like the stone of a tomb, and no one dare
put forth his arm. . . . In the time when there
were men here, they feared too, and fell upon
their faces. . . . To-day it is the woman's turn;
. . . we shall see. . . . It is time to rise at last.
. . . We know not upon what her power rests,
and I will live no longer in the shadow of her
tower. . . . Go, — go, both of you, and leave me
more alone still, if you tremble too. . . . I
shall await her. . . .

BELLANGÈRE.

Sister, I do not know what must be done, but
I stay with thee. . . .

AGLOVALE.

I too stay, my daughter. For a long time
my soul has been restless. . . . You are going to
try. . . . We have tried more than once. . . .

14

YGRAINE.

You have tried . . . you too?

AGLOVALE.

They have all tried. . . . But at the last moment they have lost their strength. . . . You will see, you too. . . . Should she order me to come up to her this very night, I should clasp both my hands without a word ; and my tired feet would climb the stair, without delay and without haste, well as I know no one comes down again with open eyes. . . . I have no more courage against her. . . . Our hands are of no use and reach no one. . . . They are not the hands we need, and all is useless. . . . But I would help you, because you hope. . . . Shut the doors, my child. Wake Tintagiles ; encircle him with your little naked arms and take him on your knees. . . . We have no other defence. . . .

ACT THIRD.

The same. YGRAINE *and* AGLOVALE *discovered.*

YGRAINE.

I have been to all the doors. There are three.
We will guard the largest. . . . The other two are
thick and low. They never open. Their keys
were lost long ago, and the iron bars are bedded
fast in the walls. Help me shut this; it is
heavier than the gate of a city. . . . It is strong,
too, and the thunder itself could not enter. . .
Are you ready for everything?

AGLOVALE (*seating himself on the threshold*).

I shall sit on the steps of the threshold, with
the sword on my knees. . . . Methinks it is not
the first time I have watched and waited here,
my child; and there are moments when we do
not understand all we remember. . . . I have
done these things, I know not when; . . . but
I never dared draw my sword. . . . To-day it
is there, before me, although my arms have no
more strength; but I will try. . . . Perhaps it is
time to defend ourselves, although we do not
understand. . . .

BELLANGÈRE, *carrying* TINTAGILES, *enters from the adjoining room.*

BELLANGÈRE.

He was awake. . . .

YGRAINE.

He is pale. . . . Why, what is the matter?

BELLANGÈRE.

I do not know. . . . He was crying silently. . . .

YGRAINE.

Tintagiles. . . .

BELLANGÈRE.

He looks the other way. . . .

YGRAINE.

He does not recognize me. . . . Tintagiles, where art thou? — It is thy sister speaking to thee. . . . What lookest thou at there? — Turn back this way. . . . Come, we will play. . . .

TINTAGILES.

No. . . . No. . . .

YGRAINE.

Thou wouldst not play?

TINTAGILES.

I can no longer walk, sister Ygraine. . . .

YGRAINE.

Thou canst no longer walk? . . . Come, come, what ails thee? — Art thou in pain a little? . . .

TINTAGILES.

Yes. . . .

YGRAINE.

Where is the pain, then? — Tell me, Tintagiles, and I will cure thee. . . .

TINTAGILES.

I can't tell, sister Ygraine, it is everywhere. . . .

YGRAINE.

Come here, Tintagiles. . . . Thou knowest my arms are gentler, and one is cured quickly there. . . . Give him to me, Bellangère. . . . He shall sit on my knees, and it will go away. . . . There, thou seest how it is! . . . Thy great sisters are here. . . . They are about thee; . . . we will defend thee, and no harm can come. . . .

TINTAGILES.

It is there, sister Ygraine. . . . Why is there no light, sister Ygraine?

YGRAINE.

There is, my child. . . . Thou dost not see the lamp that hangs down from the vault?

TINTAGILES.

Yes, yes. . . . It is not big. . . . There are no others?

YGRAINE.

Why should there be others? We can see all
we need see. . . .

TINTAGILES.

Ah ! . . .

YGRAINE.

Oh, thine eyes are deep ! . . .

TINTAGILES.

Thine too, sister Ygraine. . . .

YGRAINE.

I had not noticed it this morning. . . . I saw
arise . . . one never knows just what the soul
believes it sees. . . .

TINTAGILES.

I have not seen the soul, sister Ygraine. . . .
Why is Aglovale there on the threshold?

YGRAINE.

He is resting a little. . . . He wanted to kiss
thee before he went to bed. . . . He was waiting for thee to wake. . . .

TINTAGILES.

What is that on his knees?

YGRAINE.

On his knees? I see nothing on his knees. . . .

TINTAGILES.

Yes, yes, there is something. . . .

AGLOVALE.

Nothing much, my child. . . . I was looking at my old sword ; and I hardly recognized it. . . . It has served me many years ; but for some time I have lost all faith in it, and I think it will soon break. . . . There, by the hilt, there is a little spot. . . . I have observed the steel was growing paler, and I asked myself . . . I know not any longer what I asked. . . . My soul is very heavy to-day. . . . How can it be helped ? . . . We have to live in expectation of the unexpected. . . . And then we have to act as if we hoped. . . . There are those heavy evenings when the uselessness of life rises in the throat; and you would like to close your eyes. . . . It is late, and I am tired. . . .

TINTAGILES.

He is wounded, sister Ygraine. . . .

YGRAINE.

Where ?

TINTAGILES.

On the forehead and the hands. . . .

AGLOVALE.

Those are very old wounds that do not hurt me any more, my child. . . . It must be the light falling on them to-night. . . . Thou hast never noticed them till now ?

TINTAGILES.

He looks sad, sister Ygraine. . . .

YGRAINE.

No, no ; he is not sad, but very weary. . . .

TINTAGILES.

Thou art sad too, sister Ygraine. . . .

YGRAINE.

Why, no ; why, no ; you see, I am smiling. . . .

TINTAGILES.

And my other sister, too. . . .

YGRAINE.

Why, no ; she is smiling, too. . . .

TINTAGILES.

That is not smiling. . . . I know. . . .

YGRAINE.

Come ; kiss me and think of something else. . . . [*She kisses him.*]

TINTAGILES.

What else, sister Ygraine? — Why dost thou hurt me when thou dost kiss me so?

YGRAINE.

I hurt thee?

TINTAGILES.

Yes. . . . I don't know why I hear thy heart beat, sister Ygraine. . . .

YGRAINE.

Thou hearest it beat?

TINTAGILES.

Oh! oh! it beats, it beats, as if it would . . .

YGRAINE.

What?

TINTAGILES.

I don't know, sister Ygraine. . . .

YGRAINE.

Thou must not be alarmed without reason, nor speak in riddles. . . . Stop! thine eyes are wet. . . . Why art thou troubled? I hear thy heart beat, too. . . . You always hear it when you kiss so. . . . It is then it speaks and says things the tongue knows not of. . . .

TINTAGILES.

I did not hear it just now. . . .

YGRAINE.

Because then . . . Oh! but thine! . . . Why, what ails it? . . . It is bursting! . . .

TINTAGILES (*crying*).

Sister Ygraine! sister Ygraine!

YGRAINE.

What?

TINTAGILES.

I heard! . . . They . . . they are coming!

YGRAINE.

They, who? . . . Why, what's the matter? . . .

TINTAGILES.

The door! the door! They were there! . . .
[*He falls backward on* YGRAINE'S *knees.*

YGRAINE.

Why, what's the matter? . . . He has . . .
he has fainted. . . .

BELLANGÈRE.

Take care; . . . take care! . . . He will
fall. . . .

AGLOVALE.

[*Rising abruptly, sword in hand.*] I hear
too; . . . some one is walking in the corridor.

YGRAINE.

Oh! . . .

[*A silence — they listen.*

AGLOVALE.

I hear. . . . There is a crowd of them. . . .

YGRAINE.

A crowd! . . . What crowd?

AGLOVALE.

I do not know ; . . . you hear and you do not hear. . . . They do not walk like other beings, but they come. . . . They are touching the door. . . .

YGRAINE.

[*Clasping* TINTAGILES *convulsively in her arms.*] Tintagiles ! . . . Tintagiles ! . . .

BELLANGÈRE.

[*Kissing him at the same time.*]   I too ! . . . I too ! . . . Tintagiles ! . . .

AGLOVALE.

They are shaking the door . . . listen . . . soft ! . . . They are whispering. . . .
    [*A key is heard grating in the lock.*

YGRAINE.

They have the key ! . . .

AGLOVALE.

Yes ; . . . yes. . . . I was sure of it. . . . Wait. . . .
    [*He posts himself, with raised sword, on the last step. — To the two sisters :*]
Come ! . . . come, too ! . . .

    [A silence. The door opens a little. Trembling like the needle of a compass, Aglovale puts his sword across the opening, sticking the point of it between the beams of the door-case. The sword breaks with a crash under the ominous pressure of the folding-door, and its fragments roll echoing down the steps. Ygraine leaps up with Tintagiles, still in a faint, in her arms; and she, Bellangère and Aglovale, with vain and mighty efforts, try to push back the door, which continues to open slowly, although no one is heard or seen. Only a brightness, cold and calm, pierces into the room. At this moment, Tintagiles, suddenly straightening up, comes to himself, utters a long cry of deliverance and kisses his sister, while at the very moment of this cry, the door, resisting no longer, shuts abruptly under their pressure, which they have not had time to interrupt.]

YGRAINE.

Tintagiles ! . . .
[*They look at each other in amazement.*

AGLOVALE (*listening at the door*).

I no longer hear a sound. . . .

YGRAINE (*wild with joy*).

Tintagiles ! Tintagiles ! . . . See ! See ! . . . He is saved ! . . . See his eyes ! . . . you can see the blue. . . . He is going to speak. . . . They saw we were watching. . . . They did not dare ! . . . Kiss us ! . . . Kiss us, I tell thee ! . . . Kiss us ! . . . All ! all ! . . . To the very depths of our souls ! . . .
[*All four, with eyes filled with tears, remain closely embraced.*]

ACT FOURTH.

[A corridor before the apartment of the preceding act. Enter, veiled, three handmaids of the Queen.]

FIRST HANDMAID (*listening at the door*).

They watch no longer. . . .

SECOND HANDMAID.

It was useless to wait. . . .

THIRD HANDMAID.

She preferred that it should be done in silence. . . .

FIRST HANDMAID.

I knew that they must sleep. . . .

SECOND HANDMAID.

Open quickly. . . .

THIRD HANDMAID.

It is time. . . .

FIRST HANDMAID.

Wait at the door. I will go in alone. It is needless to be three. . . .

SECOND HANDMAID.

It is true, he is very little. . . .

THIRD HANDMAID.

You must be on your guard for the elder sister. . . .

SECOND HANDMAID.

You know the Queen would not that they should know. . . .

FIRST HANDMAID.

Fear nothing ; I am never easily heard. . . .

SECOND HANDMAID.

Go in, then ; it is time.
[*The first handmaid opens the door prudently and enters the room.*]

It is nearly midnight. . . .

THIRD HANDMAID.

Ah ! . . .
[*A silence. The first handmaid comes back from the apartment.*]

SECOND HANDMAID.

Where is he ?

FIRST HANDMAID.

He is asleep between his sisters. His arms are about their necks ; and their arms are about him, too. . . . I could not do it alone. . . .

SECOND HANDMAID.

I will go help you. . . .

THIRD HANDMAID.

Yes; go in together. . . . I will watch here. . . .

FIRST HANDMAID.

Take care; they are aware of something. . . . They are all three struggling with a bad dream. . . .

[*The two handmaids enter the room.*

THIRD HANDMAID.

They are always aware; but they do not understand. . . .

[*A silence. The first two handmaids come back again from the apartment.*]

Well?

SECOND HANDMAID.

You must come too; . . . we cannot detach them. . . .

FIRST HANDMAID.

As fast as we undo their arms, they close them on the child again. . . .

SECOND HANDMAID.

And the child clings to them harder and harder. . . .

FIRST HANDMAID.

He is resting with his forehead on the elder sister's heart. . . .

SECOND HANDMAID.

And his head rises and falls on her breasts. . . .

FIRST HANDMAID.

We shall not succeed in opening his hands the least. . . .

SECOND HANDMAID.

They plunge to the very depths of his sisters' hair. . . .

FIRST HANDMAID.

He clenches a golden curl between his little teeth. . . .

SECOND HANDMAID.

The hair of the elder will have to be cut off. . . .

FIRST HANDMAID.

The other sister's as well, you will see. . . .

SECOND HANDMAID.

Have you your shears?

THIRD HANDMAID.

Yes. . . .

FIRST HANDMAID.

Come quick ; they stir already.

SECOND HANDMAID.

Their hearts and eyelids beat in the same time. . . .

FIRST HANDMAID.

It is true; I caught a glimpse of the blue eyes of the elder. . . .

SECOND HANDMAID.

She looked at us, but saw us not. . . .

FIRST HANDMAID.

When one of them is touched, the other two start. . . .

SECOND HANDMAID.

They struggle without being able to move. . . .

FIRST HANDMAID.

The elder would have cried out, but she could not. . . .

SECOND HANDMAID.

Come quickly; they look warned. . . .

THIRD HANDMAID.

The old man is not there?

FIRST HANDMAID.

Yes; but he sleeps in a corner. . . .

SECOND HANDMAID.

He sleeps with his forehead on the pommel of his sword.

FIRST HANDMAID.

He is aware of nothing; and he does not dream. . . .

THIRD HANDMAID.

Come, come ; we must have done with it. . . .

FIRST HANDMAID.

You will have trouble untangling their limbs. . . .

SECOND HANDMAID.

True ; they are intertwined like those of the drowned. . . .

THIRD HANDMAID.

Come, come. . . .
[They enter the room. A great silence, broken by sighs and dull murmurs of an anguish smothered by sleep. Afterwards, the three handmaids come out in all haste from the sombre apartment. One of them carries Tintagiles asleep in her arms, his little hands and mouth shrivelled with sleep and agony, and flooding him all over with the flowing of long golden locks ravished from the two sisters' hair. They flee in silence until, when they come to the end of the corridor, Tintagiles, suddenly waking, utters a great cry of supreme distress.]

TINTAGILES (*from the depths of the corridor*).

A-ah ! . . .
[New silence. Then the two sisters are heard, in the next room, waking and rising uneasily.]

YGRAINE (*in the room*).

Tintagiles ! . . . Where is he ? . . .

BELLANGÈRE.

He is no longer here. . . .

YGRAINE (*with increasing anguish*).

Tintagiles ! . . . A lamp ! a lamp ! . . . Light it ! . . .

BELLANGÈRE.

Yes . . . yes ! . . .

YGRAINE.

[She is seen, through the open door, coming forward within the room, with a lamp in her hand.]

The door is wide open !

THE VOICE OF TINTAGILES (*almost inaudible in the distance*).

Sister Ygraine ! . . .

YGRAINE.

He cries ! . . . he cries ! . . . Tintagiles ! Tintagiles ! . . .

[She rushes headlong into the corridor. Bellangère tries to follow her, but faints on the steps of the threshold.]

ACT FIFTH.

A great iron door beneath gloomy arches. Enter YGRAINE, *haggard, dishevelled, with a lamp in her hand.*

YGRAINE.

[*Turning back wildly.*] They have not followed me. . . . Bellangère ! . . . Bellangère ! . . . Aglovale ! . . . Where are they? — They said they loved him, and they have left me all alone ! . . . Tintagiles ! . . . Tintagiles ! . . . Oh ! it is true. . . . I have climbed up, I have climbed up innumerable steps between great pitiless walls, and my heart can no longer sustain me. . . . The arches seem to stir. . . . [*She leans against the pillars of an arch.*] I shall fall. . . . Oh ! oh ! my poor life ! I feel it. . . . It is at the very edge of my lips, trying to get away. . . . I do not know what I have done. . . . I have seen nothing ; I have heard nothing. . . . Oh, the silence ! . . . I found all these golden curls along the steps and along the walls ; and I followed them. I picked them up. . . . Oh ! oh ! they are very beautiful ! Little thumbkin ! . . . little thumbkin ! . . . What did I say? I remember. . . . I do not believe in it, either ; . . . one can sleep. . . . All that is of no consequence, and it is not possible. . . . I do not know what I think any longer. . . . One is waked up, and then . . . At bottom, come, at bottom,

one must reflect. . . . They say this, they say
that ; but the soul — that follows another road
altogether. You do not know all you unloose.
I came here with my little lamp. . . . It was not
blown out in spite of the wind in the stairway. . . .
At bottom, what must be thought of it? There
are too many things unsettled. . . . And yet there
are some who should know them ; but why do
they not speak? [*Looking about her.*] I have
never seen all this. . . . One may not climb so
high ; everything is forbidden. . . . It is cold. . . .
It is so dark, too, one might fear to breathe. . . .
They say the shadows poison. . . . Yonder door
is fearful. . . . [*She approaches the door and
gropes over it.*] Oh! it is cold! . . . It is of
smooth iron ; all smooth, and has no lock. . . .
Where does it open, then? I see no hinges. . . .
I believe it is embedded in the wall. . . . One can
go no higher ; . . . there are no more steps. . . .
[*Uttering a terrible cry.*] Ah! . . . still more
golden curls, shut in the door! . . . Tintagiles!
Tintagiles! . . . I heard the door fall to just
now! . . . I remember! I remember! . . . It
must! . . . [*She beats frantically with fist and
feet on the door.*] Oh! the monster! the monster! . . . You are here! . . . Listen! I blaspheme! I blaspheme and spit at you! . . .

> [Knocking, in tiny strokes, heard on the other
> side of the door ; then the voice of Tintagiles
> pierces, very feebly, through the iron
> barriers.]

TINTAGILES.

Sister Ygraine, sister Ygraine !

YGRAINE.

Tintagiles ! . . . What ? . . . What ? . . . Tintagiles, is it thou ? . . .

TINTAGILES.

Open quickly, open quickly ! . . . She is there ! . . .

YGRAINE.

Oh ! oh ! . . . Who ? . . . Tintagiles, my little Tintagiles ! . . . dost thou hear me ? . . . What is it ! . . . What has happened ? . . . Tintagiles ! . . . Thou hast not been hurt ? . . . Where art thou ? . . . Art thou there ? . . .

TINTAGILES.

Sister Ygraine, sister Ygraine ! . . . I shall die if thou dost not open me the door. . . .

YGRAINE.

Wait ; I am trying ; wait. . . . I am opening it, I am opening it. . . .

TINTAGILES.

But thou dost not understand me ! . . . Sister Ygraine ! . . . There is no time ! . . . She could not hold me. . . . I struck her, struck her. . . . I ran. . . . Quick, quick, she is here ! . . .

YGRAINE.

I am coming, I am coming. . . . Where is she ?

TINTAGILES.

I see nothing, . . . but I hear . . . oh! I am
afraid, sister Ygraine, I am afraid! . . . Quick,
quick! . . . Open quickly! . . . for the love of
the dear God, sister Ygraine! . . .

YGRAINE (*groping over the door anxiously*).

I am sure to find . . . wait a little . . . a minute . . . a moment . . .

TINTAGILES.

I cannot wait any longer, sister Ygraine. . . .
She is breathing behind me. . . .

YGRAINE.

It is nothing, Tintagiles; my little Tintagiles,
don't be afraid. . . . It is because I cannot
see. . . .

TINTAGILES.

Yes, thou canst; I see thy light plainly. . . .
It is light by thee, sister Ygraine. . . . Here I
can see no longer. . . .

YGRAINE.

Thou seest me, Tintagiles? Where can one
see? There is no chink. . . .

TINTAGILES.

Yes, yes, there is one, but it is so little! . . .

YGRAINE

Which side? Here? . . . Tell me, tell me!
. . . There, perhaps?

TINTAGILES.

Here, here. . . . Dost thou not hear? I am knocking. . . .

YGRAINE.

Here?

TINTAGILES.

Higher. . . . But it is so little! . . . One could not pass a needle through it! . . .

YGRAINE.

Don't be afraid; I shall be there. . . .

TINTAGILES.

Oh, I hear, sister Ygraine! . . . Pull! Pull! Thou must pull! She is here! . . . if thou couldst open it a little . . . just a little. . . . I am so tiny! . . .

YGRAINE.

I have no nails left, Tintagiles. . . . I have pulled, I have pushed, I have pounded! . . . I have pounded! . . . [*She pounds again and tries to shake the immovable door.*] Two of my fingers are numb. . . . Do not weep; . . . it is iron. . . .

TINTAGILES (*sobbing desperately*).

Thou hast nothing to open it with, sister Ygraine? . . . Nothing at all, nothing at all; . . . and I could go through; . . . for I am so little, so little. . . . Thou knowest well. . . .

YGRAINE.

I have nothing but my lamp, Tintagiles. . . . There! There! . . . [*She beats hard on the*

*door, with the help of her lamp of clay, which
goes out and is broken.*]   Oh! . . . Everything
is dark all at once! . . . Tintagiles, where art
thou? . . . Oh, listen, listen! . . . Thou canst
not open it from within? . . .

TINTAGILES.

No, no; there is n't anything. . . . I can't
feel anything at all. . . . I can't see the little
bright chink any longer. . . .

YGRAINE.

What ails thee, Tintagiles? . . . I hardly
hear any longer. . . .

TINTAGILES.

Little sister, sister Ygraine. . . . It is no longer
possible. . . .

YGRAINE.

What is it, Tintagiles? . . . Where goest
thou? . . .

TINTAGILES.

She is there! . . . I have no more courage. —
Sister Ygraine, sister Ygraine! . . . I feel her! . . .

YGRAINE.

Who? . . . Who? . . .

TINTAGILES.

I do not know. . . . I do not see. . . . But it
is no longer possible! . . . She . . . she is taking
me by the throat. . . . She has put her hand on
my throat. . . . Oh! oh! sister Ygraine, come
here. . . .

YGRAINE.

Yes, yes. . . .

TINTAGILES.

It is so dark ! . . .

YGRAINE.

Struggle, defend thyself, tear her ! . . . Don't
be afraid. . . . One moment ! . . . I shall be
there. . . . Tintagiles ! . . . Tintagiles ! answer
me ! . . . Help ! . . . Where art thou ? . . . I
am going to help thee. . . . Kiss me . . . through
the door . . . here . . . here. . . .

TINTAGILES (*very feebly*).

Here . . . here . . . sister Ygraine. . . .

YGRAINE.

It is here, it is here I am giving kisses, hearest
thou ?   Again ! again ! . . .

TINTAGILES (*more and more feebly*).

I am giving them, too . . . here . . . sister
Ygraine ! . . . sister Ygraine ! . . . Oh ! . . .
      [*The fall of a little body is heard behind
          the iron door.*]

YGRAINE.

Tintagiles ! . . . Tintagiles ! . . . What hast
thou done ? . . . Give him up ! give him up ! . . .
for the love of God, give him up ! . . . I no
longer hear. . . . — What have you done with
him ? . . . Do him no harm, will you ? . . . It

is only a poor child ! . . . He does not resist. . . .
See, see. . . . I am not wicked. . . . I have gone
down on both knees. . . . Give him up, I pray
thee. . . . It is not for myself alone, thou
knowest. . . . I will do all one could wish. . . .
I am not bad, you see. . . . I beseech you with
clasped hands. . . . I was wrong. . . . I sub-
mit utterly, thou seest well. . . . I have lost all
I had. . . . Let me be punished some other
way. . . . There are so many things that could
give me more pain . . . if thou lovest to give
pain. . . . Thou wilt see. . . . But this poor
child has done nothing. . . . What I said was
not true . . . but I did not know. . . . I know
well you are very good. . . . One must forgive
in the end ! . . . He is so young, he is so beautiful, and he is so little ! . . . You see, it is not possible ! . . . He puts his little arms about your
neck, his little mouth on your mouth ; and God
himself could not resist any longer. . . . You
will open, will you not ? . . . I ask almost nothing. . . . I should only have him a moment,
one little moment. . . . I do not remember . . .
thou understandest. . . . I did not have time. . . .
There needs hardly anything to let him pass. . . .
It is not hard. . . . [*A long inexorable silence.*] —
Monster ! . . . Monster ! . . . I spit —. . . !

> [*She sinks down and continues to sob
> softly, with her arms stretched up on
> the door, in the darkness.*]

[CURTAIN.]

PRINTED BY R. R. DONNELLEY
AND SONS COMPANY AT THE
LAKESIDE PRESS, CHICAGO, ILL.